MIME, UUENCODE & ZIP

MIME, UUENCODE & ZIP

JUDI FERNANDEZ

A Subsidiary of
Henry Holt and Co., Inc.

MIS:Press
A Subsidiary of Henry Holt and Company, Inc.
115 West 18th Street
New York, New York 10011
http://www.mispress.com

First Edition—1997

ISBN: 1-55828-528-8

10 9 8 7 6 5 4 3 2 1

Associate Publisher: *Paul Farrell*

Managing Editor: *Shari Chappell*   **Editor:** *Michael Sprague*
Technical Editor: *Michael Funduc*   **Production Editor:** *Maya Riddick*

Dedication

This book is fondly dedicated to my dear friend Karla von Huben, who has had to put up with a lot while I was writing it. Karla is mentioned several times in here, but only she knows where. :)

Acknowledgements

My thanks to Mike Funduc of Funduc Software, not only for letting me include his handy shell extension program on the disk that accompanies this book, but also for helping me through some of the stickier technical points on data encoding. Thanks also to Michael Sprague, my long-suffering editor at MIS:Press, who worked long and hard on this book, and who only cracked the whip on occasion and always with good humor.

I'd also like to thank all the wonderful people who give me support, guidance, counseling, and occasionally, diversion: my wonderful husband Paul Knudsen (who has dines on a lot of pizza while I was busy writing this), my cybersisters Cpierce976, EWGRED, JudiMaf, OLYVE FOUR, and Whissperss, and my biological sisters Doris Northrup and Donna Tabler. Without them, I could not have written this book (or anything else).

Contents-In-Brief

CONTENTS

Chapter 5: Downloading Files from the World Wide Web . . .61

Chapter 6: Downloading from FTP, Gopher, and Usenet . .79

PART III: WORKING WITH COMPRESSION AND ENCODING PROGRAMS

PART IV: COMPUTER VIRUSES

PART V: CHECKLISTS

PREFACE

If you've ever used the Internet—and that includes online services such as America Online, CompuServe, AT&T WorldNet, and Prodigy—you know that you're in contact with millions of people every day. Perhaps billions. And they are all exchanging information at a rate that Federal Express never dreamed of.

But sometimes all does not work perfectly in "cyberia," especially when you're trying to exchange files with people. The file you send to a friend might never get there. Or when it does arrive, it appears to be garbled. Maybe you download a program from FTP, but you can't figure out how to run it because its extension is .zip instead of .exe. You might want to download some graphics from a newsgroup, but all you can find is messages containing nonsense text—where are the graphics?

This book will help you solve these problems. It explains why data on the Internet is *compressed* and *encoded*, not garbled—it might even be split into several segments. And you'll learn how to turn it back into useful information again by decompressing, decoding, and reassembling it. It also shows you how to compress, encode, and split files yourself, not just to save online time but also to increase the chances of your data arriving safely at its destination.

T I P   The disk at the back of this book includes the software you need for compressing, decompressing, encoding, and decoding files. You'll also find a certificate for $5 off the price of the latest version of WinZip, the most popular compression utility for Windows.

1

And because you increase your risks when you download files from email and other Internet resources, I have also included a section on viruses on the Internet. You'll learn what they are (and aren't), how to avoid them, how to detect them, and how to deal with them. Most importantly, I hope, you'll learn not to panic at every media-hyped virus scare—instead you'll know how to calmly assess the real dangers of infection and how to avoid it.

To tell the truth, I went a little beyond what this book is supposed to be about. (Don't tell my editor!) It is supposed to deal with files before you upload them and after you download them, but I couldn't stop myself from including information on the uploading and downloading processes, too. So you'll find step-by-step instructions on how to upload and download files via email, the World Wide Web, FTP, Usenet (newsgroups), and even Gopher using several of the most popular Internet applications, such as America Online, Netscape, and Eudora. You'll find some procedures built into the chapters in Part II, but most of them are in Part V, which is simply a collection of checklists for a variety of procedures.

WHO IS THIS BOOK FOR?

I wrote this book for PC users (not Macintosh) who want to use the Internet but have not yet learned how to compress, decompress, encode, and decode files. I assumed very little background knowledge. I assumed, for example, that you know what the Internet is, at least in a general way, but that you don't know what compression and encoding are.

This doesn't mean Mac users won't get a lot out of this book. The compression and encoding technologies discussed are universal and a great deal of cross-platform information is covered. Also, the Internet is more and more becoming platform independent. The major utilities discussed in the book are PC, Windows, and Windows 95 specific, but Mac users are going to run into these file formats as well.

You might already know parts of what this book teaches. Lots of people, for example, know how to deal with a **.zip** file but not a **.sit** or **.uue** file. Then you might want to read just the introduction to each chapter. It includes a detailed list of the topics covered, which gives you a chance to decide quickly whether or not you need to read that chapter.

ABOUT THE AUTHOR

When I was in college, my dorm mates hung a sign on my door that said, "Judi is in love with an IBM 650 with curly blond control wires and baby blue panel lights." It was true. My love affair with computers and technology continues unabated. Nowadays, I'm in love with, first and foremost, my wonderful husband Paul, whom I met in an online chat room. He shares my love of computers, and since you can never completely catch up with all there is to know about computers and "cyberia," I'm sure we will have plenty to talk about and to work towards for the rest of our days.

When I entered the world of computers, I quickly discovered that my niche was in writing manuals, online help, self-study guides, multimedia courses, and other learning materials to help people use these wonderful tools. I have now published over 40[1] how-to books like this one. Some have won awards for technical communication; a few have even hit the computer best seller list—which isn't the same as the New York Times best seller list, but it makes me happy. My specialty is explaining complex topics in language that my 12-year-old daughter can understand.[2]

By the way, that sign was hung on my door in 1959, when I was 18 years old. I first fell in love with computers when I was 16 and took a programming class at IBM. I've been working with and studying computers ever since. That's the basis for my claim that I was the first teenage computer nerd. If you know a teen who started earlier than 1957, please let me know. I would somewhat regretfully hand over my title to him or her.

My Web Pages

I publish a web site full of daily tips on using America Online, Windows 95, Microsoft Word 7.0 for Windows 95, Microsoft Works 4.0 for Windows 95, HTML, and the Web. Some of the tips link to complete lessons on a particular topic, such as how to use AOL's address book. You'll find my Tips and WebLessons site at http://members.aol.com/judinorth.

I also maintain a site for my book readers. It contains additional information for my current books, links to software, and anything else that I think is pertinent. You'll find this site at http://members.aol.com/jnfbooks.

---

[1] I confess it, I've lost count.

[2] She's 26 now, and a mother herself, but I still try to explain things to that 12 year old she used to be.

PART I

Archiving and Encoding Technology

CHAPTER 1

Data Compression, Archiving, and PKZip

Suppose that you want to send your new Internet buddy some photos of you on your Harley Hog. You scan the pictures, creating four TIFF image files totaling about a 1.5 megabytes of data. It takes 15 minutes to upload the files to your friend. It takes him even longer to download them because his modem is slower. You could have saved your friend and yourself some expensive online time by archiving and compressing those files. The four TIFF files could compress down to a single file of 100K, taking less than a minute to upload and download—and no data is lost! That's what this chapter is about.

What you'll learn in this chapter:

- What compression is and why we need it
- What archiving is and why we need it
- How PKZip compresses and archives data
- What self-extracting files are and why we need them
- A warning about bogus PKZip programs that could harm your system
- Some other products based on PKZip's compression format

- Some other popular compression programs, including StuffIt for the Mac, compress for UNIX systems, and Stacker
- File formats that are already compressed, such as .gif, .jpg, and .mpg
- How your modem compresses data
- The difference between lossy and lossless compression

WHAT IS DATA COMPRESSION?

Data compression is a process that makes a computer file take up less space by removing extraneous data from it. How can any data be extraneous? Let's take a fairly simple, but real, example. A monochrome graphics file stores one byte for every pixel in the image. If you could read the data, it would look like this: *black black black black white white black black black white white white white*, and so on. A simple data compression scheme would reduce that string of information to *black 4 white 2 black 3 white 4*, thus reducing 13 bytes to 8. A more complex scheme like PKZip's can safely reduce a file like this by more than 95 percent.

Table 1.1 shows typical savings for some common types of files.

Table 1.1 Typical Compression Ratios with PKZip

File Type	Typical Ratio
Uncompressed graphics (.**bmp, .tif**)	95%
Spreadsheet	80%
Database	75%
Text	65%
Executable Program	50%
Compressed graphics (.**gif, .jpg**)	Negligible

The reasons for compressing data aren't hard to figure out. For one, it saves space on your disks, a boon if you don't yet measure your hard disk space in gigabytes or when you're trying to fit a large spreadsheet on a floppy to take to a meeting. But even more important for the subject of this book, compressed files take less time to upload and download via the Internet. The less time they take, the less money they cost for both the sender and the receiver. And as a side benefit, there's less chance your job will get dumped in midstream.

A file can't be used in compressed format. A compressed program can't be run, a compressed graphic can't be displayed, and a compressed document can't be edited or printed. You have to *decompress* the file before you can use it. Decompression restores the data that was removed by compression.

Compressing and decompressing take time, but you do it offline so the time doesn't cost you very much. The online time that you save by transferring compressed files more than compensates for the extra time you spend compressing and decompressing offline.

NOTE   The .**gif** and .**jpg** formats were designed for Internet use and are already compressed. No further compression is necessary. They are automatically compressed and decompressed by any program capable of handling them.

PKZip: The Universal Compression Tool

By far the most popular compression program in the PC world (as opposed to the Macintosh and UNIX worlds) is PKZip by PKWare. (The initials *PK* belong to its developer, Phil Katz.) It would be not be exaggerating to say that PKZip is nearly universal among PCs, due in part to its excellence and in part to the fact that it is distributed as shareware.

NOTE

Shareware means that you can get a copy from a friend or an online service, try it out for a while, and pay for it only if you decide to keep it. Unfortunately, too many people treat shareware like freeware—they never send in that payment. And so, you'll often find shareware with a built-in time limit. When the time limit expires, so does the software

The words *PKZip*, *zip*, *PKUnzip*, and *unzip* have become synonymous with compression and decompression for PC users.

WARNING

Be careful where you get PKZip. Because this program is so popular and is distributed as shareware, some hackers have created bogus versions that could contain viruses that will harm your system, perhaps wiping out your hard drive. In particular, be wary of any program promising to be the new PKZip 3.0. The latest release of PKZip is 2.04; any version newer than that is a fake. I have included a copy of PKZIP 2.04 on the disk that accompanies this book.

How PKZip Compresses Data

How does PKZip work? Let's start with a simple example, the phrase *The Trouble with Tribbles*. First, let's strike out any repeated string of three or more characters. (Spaces count as characters in compression technology, so I've printed them as ^ to make them clearer.)

```
T h e ^  T r o u b l e ^  w i t  h ^ T r i b b l e s
```

Even in this short phrase, we found two repeated strings. When we compress the phrase, we replace the repeats with *tokens* indicating which characters should be repeated. In the following phrase, the token [4,3] refers back to the fourth character (which is a ^) for a length of three characters (^ T r).

```
T h e ^  T r o u b l e ^ w i t h  [4,3]  i b  [9,3]  s
```

If each token takes two bytes, we have compressed this phrase from 25 bytes to 23 without losing any essential information. A decompressor such as PKUnzip can easily replace the tokens with the original strings, reproducing the original phrase. No data is lost by the compression/decompression process.

NOTE I considered only repeats of three or more characters in this example because the token requires two bytes. Replacing one or two characters with a token would not save any space, so three characters is the minimum replacement. In some settings, the tokens take three or four bytes, so the minimum replacement must be four or five bytes long.

We saved two whole bytes. That's a compression factor of eight percent. We don't see much savings here because this example is so short. But few files are only 25 bytes long. Watch what happens with the first portion of Lincoln's Gettysburg Address:

```
F o u r s c o r e ^ a n d ^ s e v e n ^ y e a r s ^ a g o
^ o u r ^ f a t h e r s ^ b r o u g h t ^ f o r t h ^ u p
o n ^ t h i s ^ c o n t i n e n t ^ a ^ n e w ^ n a t i o
n , ^ c o n c e i v e d ^ i n ^ l i b e r t y ^ a n d ^ d
e d i c a t e d ^ t o ^ t h e ^ p r o p o s i t i o n ^ t
h a t ^ a l l ^ m e n ^ a r e ^ c r e a t e d ^ e q u a l
. ^ N o w ^ w e ^ a r e ^ e n g a g e d ^ i n ^ a ^ g r e
a t ^ c i v i l ^ w a r , ^ t e s t i n g ^ w h e t h e r
^ t h a t ^ n a t i o n , ^ o r ^ a n y ^ n a t i o n ^ s
o ^ c o n c e i v e d ^ a n d ^ s o ^ d e d i c a t e d ,
^ c a n ^ l o n g ^ e n d u r e .
```

By the end of this short example, you can see that the repeats are getting not only more frequent, but also longer. You would see this trend become even more apparent if we continued to the end of the speech. Here we reduced 307 bytes to 240, for a compression factor of 22 percent.

ARCHIVING WITH PKZIP

PKZip not only compresses, it also *archives*—combines several files into one in such a way that they can be reliably separated again. When I send a new chapter to MIS:Press, I have to send the word processed document and the figure files, perhaps 20 or more files in all. I zip them together into one file and upload that from my place in Atlanta. A few minutes later, my editor in New York, Michael Sprague, downloads it and *extracts* the files from it. We both save a lot of time and money—not to mention hassle—by having to deal with only one file on the Internet. (Let's not even talk about older ways of sending chapters.)

NOTE   The term *extract* means that the files are separated and decompressed. It's just one step with PKUnzip (and all compatible unzipping programs). The term *zip* usually refers to the process of compressing and archiving; the term *unzip* is synonymous with *extract*.

SELF-EXTRACTING ARCHIVES

When you zip documents, you end up with a file with a **.zip** extension, as in **chap1.zip**. Most people call it a *zip file*. The person who receives the file must have some way of unzipping it. He or she has to have PKUnzip or a comparable program. But not everyone has an unzipping program. In fact, many newcomers to the Internet don't even know what a zip file is. How can you make sure that anyone who receives your file can unzip it?

The answer is you create a *self-extracting archive*. This is a program file that contains the archive along with the necessary software to unzip it. Running the self-extracting archive automatically unzips it. If you turned the archive named **chapter1.zip** into a self-extracting archive, for example, it would become an executable file named

chapter1.exe. All a recipient would have to do is double-click (or otherwise run) **chapter1.exe** to extract the files from it.

OTHER PRODUCTS BASED ON PKZIP

If you have the impression by now that Phil Katz is no dummy, you're right. And one of the smartest things he did was to release PKZip's compression scheme into the public domain. That means that anyone can use it, free of charge. So other people can write programs that can interchange files with PKZip. I could, for example, write a program that would zip and unzip files. But I'm not going to, because there are many programs out there for just that purpose.

Well, why would anyone bother to write a program that does the same thing as PKZip and PKUnzip? For one, to combine zipping and unzipping with other features, such as compressing and decompressing using other compression schemes. For another, because until recently PKZip and PKUnzip ran only under DOS, and you had to use old-fashioned DOS commands to control them. Most people today prefer Windows, and many programs have been written to let you zip and unzip files without resorting to DOS.

I have included an excellent Windows zipping and unzipping program with this book—the popular WinZip by Nico Mak Computing, Inc. I've included the 32-bit version on the disk at the back of this book: a 16-bit version that runs under Windows 3.*x* is also available from Nico Mak Computing. With the 32-bit version, you can use drag-and-drop file management and long filenames.

You'll learn how to use both PKZip and WinZip in later chapters.

T I P

MicroHelp's ExplorerPlus provides another interesting approach to handling zipped files under Windows 95. ExplorerPlus looks and behaves much like Windows 95's Explorer, but adds on several more features, including automatic zip file management. As you can see in Figure 1.1, zip files appear in the left-hand pane just as though they were folders. When you select one, you can see its contents in the right-hand pane without starting up a separate zipping or unzipping program. You can maneuver the files in the zip file just as if they were in a normal folder; for example, you can move or copy them to another program, or open, delete, and print them. ExplorerPlus zips and unzips the files as necessary, sometimes calling on your copy of PKZip or PKUnzip to do the actual work.

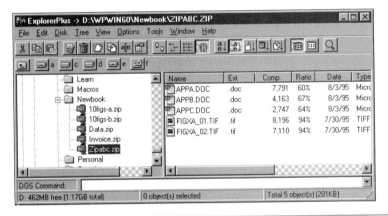

Figure 1.1 ExplorerPlus treats zip files as if they were folders.

See "Some Handy Internet Sites" at the end of this chapter for the address of MicroHelp's home page, where you can download ExplorerPlus along with its companion program called PowerDesk.

T I P

These are only a few examples of the many programs that incorporate zipping and unzipping.

A Brief Look at Some Other Compression Software

PKZip is not the only compression program. Several others are available for the PC, as well as the Macintosh, UNIX, and OS/2. You might encounter files compressed by some of these programs, so you should at least recognize them when you see them.

Table 1.2 summarizes the programs, which are explained in more detail in the following sections.

Table 1.2 Compression and Archiving Software

Filename Extension	Program	Handled by WinZip?
.arc	ARC	External*
.arj	ARJ	External†
.gz	gzip	Built-in
.lzh	LHArc	External
.sit	StuffIt	No
.sit.hqx	StuffIt and Binhex	No
.tar	tar	Built-in
.tar.z or .taz	tar and compress	Built-in
.tar.gz or .tgz	tar and gzip	Built-in
.Z	compress	Built-in
.z	gzip	Built-in
.zip	PKZip	Built-in

*External means that WinZip needs to access another program (such as ARC) to handle this file format.

†Built-in means that WinZip can handle this file format with no outside help.

Other PC Compression and Archiving Programs

ARC is an old DOS program that compresses and archives files. It produces files with the **.arc** extension, as in **tunes.arc**.

You probably won't run into many **.arc** files; but if you happen to encounter one that you want to extract, you'll need to get a program such as **ARC.EXE or PKXARC.EXE.**

TIP

You'll find "Some Handy Internet Sites" at the end of this chapter. Many of the programs listed in this section can be downloaded from those Web sites.

A new program that is growing in popularity is a Japanese program called LHarc, which produces files with the **.lzh** extension, as in **groups.lzh**. It accomplishes excellent compression ratios and is free, so you'll be finding more and more files on the Internet compressed by LHarc.

NOTE

LHArc is not just shareware, which you're supposed to pay for eventually. It is completely free.

ARJ by Robert Jung is another up-and-coming program that produces files with the **.arj** extension, as in **bouquets.arj**. ARJ is also free for noncommercial users, although commercial users must purchase a license.

Some Popular Macintosh Compression Programs

Aladdin System's shareware program called StuffIt is as popular on the Mac as PKZip is on the PC. And like PKZip, StuffIt both compresses and archives. If you encounter files with the **.sit** extension, as in **photos.sit**, they are probably compressed and archived by StuffIt.

StuffIt is capable of creating a self-extracting archive with the extension **.sea**. This Macintosh program file won't run on PCs, however.

NOTE

You might also see Mac files with two extensions, **.sit** and **.hqx**, as in **probs.sit.hqx**. These files have been encoded by BinHex after stuffing. Encoding is explained in Chapters 2 and 3.

UNIX COMPRESSION AND ARCHIVING PROGRAMS

Because the Internet originated on and still operates for the most part on minicomputers running UNIX, we're more or less stuck with dealing with UNIX-based files. Usually they will be compressed by a program called compress—with a lowercase "c." compress generates a file with extension **.Z**—an uppercase "Z." compress's counterpart is called uncompress.

compress doesn't archive, it only compresses. UNIX uses an archiving program called tar, which generates a **.tar** extension. When data has been archived first and then compressed, it has the double extension **.tar.Z**, as in **gestures.tar.Z**. Sometimes **.tar.Z** is combined into **.taz**, which is easier for DOS and Windows 3.1 to swallow.

UNIX users don't seem to mind going through multiple steps to accomplish a task.

NOTE

A newer compression program that is gaining in popularity is called gzip (pronounced *gee-zip*). It generates files with the **.gz** extension, as in **lol.gz** or **gestures.tar.gz**. Sometimes the double extension is combined into **.tgz**. The decompression twin for gzip is called gunzip (pronounced *gee-un-zip*).

gzip can also create **.z** files—the same format as compress, but with a lowercase "z." gunzip can decompress **.Z**, **.z**, and **.gz** files, as can StuffIt and WinZip.

NOTE

compress is running into some legal problems because it uses a compression scheme that may be patented by someone else, so gzip could become the primary UNIX compression program. Currently, compress is included with the UNIX operating system, whereas gzip must be added to it; but that could change soon.

CROSSING PLATFORMS: EXCHANGING FILES WITH MACINTOSH AND UNIX USERS

When you download to your PC a file that was created, compressed, and archived on a Macintosh, we say that you're "crossing platforms," from the Mac platform to the PC platform. More and more, we need to be able to cross platforms. In the old days—that is, more than a couple of years ago—the compression and archiving utilities prevented you from crossing platforms. A Mac couldn't unzip a **.zip** file, and a PC couldn't unstuff a **.sit** file, for example. But all that has changed. WinZip and StuffIt, for example, don't just handle their own file formats; they also handle many other formats from a variety of platforms.

Even when you can't extract a file with WinZip, you can probably locate and download some software to extract it, no matter what platform or software was used to compress and archive it. For example, there are programs for the PC that will unstuff **.sit** files, extract **.tar** files, and so on. You can find such programs on most online services and bulletin boards, or check "Some Handy Internet Sites" at the end of this chapter.

T I P   If you're faced with an extension such as **.cpt** and don't know what software will extract it, try the Web site called "Answers to FAQ about Compression." One of the FAQs lists as many file extensions as possible and makes available software that will extract them.

So you can see, you can share files with people who use other platforms, as far as data compression and archiving are concerned. But that doesn't mean that a another platform's file will be compatible with your system or vice versa. Neither system can run a program developed for the other, for example. Can you exchange sound and video clips, word processing documents, spreadsheets, and the like? Yes, but only if you have—or get—the right software to process those files after you extract them.

COMPRESSION VOLUMES

So far, the programs discussed compress files on an individual or group basis. You select one or more files and then run the appropriate program to compress and archive them. But there is another popular way that compression is managed by systems such as Stacker (from Stac Electronics) and DriveSpace (from Microsoft). Let's take Stacker as an example; DriveSpace is practically the same.

When you install Stacker, it creates a compression volume on your hard drive. This volume acts like a separate drive, with its own drive name. Whenever you add a file to that volume, Stacker automatically compresses it. When you read a file from the volume, Stacker automatically extracts it.

Because it all happens automatically, you don't have to be aware of the compression or extraction, unless something goes wrong. The benefit, of course, is that you can store much more data on your hard drive—perhaps up to three times as much, depending on what kinds of files you store.

NOTE   I'm not trying to sell you on Stacker or DriveSpace. There can be problems, and all that compression and extraction can slow down your system. But a discussion of the major types of compression would hardly be complete without mentioning these popular programs.

Stacker doesn't save you from compressing and archiving files to be uploaded. Because Stacker extracts them as soon as you read them from the drive, you still have to compress them with a program such as PKZip before you upload them. Similarly, if you download a compressed and archived file, you still have to extract it before you can read or use it.

MODEM COMPRESSION

Did you know that your modem is capable of automatically compressing all the data you send? If your modem adheres to the v42.bis standard, it does. The v42.bis modem at the other end automatically extracts the data again. Unfortunately, unless your modem and the modem at the other end of the phone line follow the exact same protocols, they frequently just end up sending data in an uncompressed form.

LOSSLESS AND LOSSY COMPRESSION

You might hear the terms *lossy* and *lossless* when referring to compression programs. They indicate whether any data is lost by the compression-extraction process.

Compression schemes such as PKZip's and StuffIt's are known as *lossless* because they do not allow data to be lost. With lossy compression schemes, however, some data is lost. Lossy schemes are used in cases where the damage to the product is considered affordable when compared to the savings.

Naturally, you would not use lossy compression on files containing word processing documents, spreadsheets, and other character data. But for photographs, audio clips, video clips, and other analog data, a slight loss of data does little harm. The compression schemes used for **.jpg** and **.gif** images, for example, result in lossy compression, as does the MPEG compressed video format.

SOME HANDY INTERNET SITES

PKWare, makers of PKZip and related products:

```
http://www.pkware.com/index.html
```

Aladdin Systems, makers of StuffIt:

```
http://www.aladdinsys.com/index.html
```

MicroHelp, makers of ExplorerPlus (along with a companion program called PowerDesk):

```
http://www.microhelp.com/index.html
```

General information about compression and many links to other compression sites:

```
http://www.internz.com/compression-pointers.html
```

Answers to Frequently asked questions (FAQs) about compression:

```
http://www.cis.ohio-state.edu/hypertext/faq/usenet/
compression-faq/top.html
```

What's Next?

Compression and archiving are only the first step in preparing a file for email or Usenet (that is, Internet newsgroups). If the file contains any binary data, it also needs to be encoded. That's the subject of the next two chapters.

CHAPTER 2

Encoding and uuencode

Did you know that you can email only ASCII data via the Internet? Binary data, such as software, word processing documents, spreadsheets, and graphics, can't be mailed as is, nor can it be posted on a Usenet newsgroup. (Some newer Internet features, such as FTP and the World Wide Web, can handle binary data.)

But... people mail and post those kinds of files on the Internet all the time! What gives? That's what the next two chapters are about. You have to convert binary files into ASCII files by a process called *encoding*. And that means that they must be *decoded* at the other end, of course.

In this chapter, you'll learn about encoding with a program called *uuencode*, along with similar programs. In Chapter 4, you'll learn a newer and easier method of encoding email (but not newsgroups) called *MIME*.

What you'll learn in this chapter:

- What ASCII data is
- What binary data is
- Why we can't transmit binary data via email
- How uuencode works (and uudecode too)
- Why some encoded files are split into parts
- What xxencode is and why we need it

ASCII AND BINARY DATA

We'll get into some of the details of encoding and decoding later, but first let's look at exactly what ASCII data is and how it differs from binary data.

A computer is basically a numerical device. It handles numbers quite naturally; but how does it handle characters such as letters, symbols, and the digits used in phone numbers, addresses, and so on? It uses a numeric code to represent the characters. A primitive code, for example, might use the numbers 1 through 26 to represent A through Z, 27 through 52 to represent a through z, 53 through 62 for the ten digits, and 63 through 100 for a collection of symbols.

In the early days of computers, each manufacturer came up with its own character code. The number *10* might represent a *J* on one computer, a * on another computer, and a *c* on a third computer. That was fine for companies with only one computer and no need to exchange data with other organizations; but for the government, the military, and large corporations, it was unacceptable. If you tried to transport character data from one computer to another, you got garbage—and chaos.

Enter the American National Standards Institute (ANSI), the organization responsible for setting standards for such things as weights, measures, and time. They devised the American Standard Code for Information Interchange (ASCII). When most computer manufacturers adopted the ASCII code, their computers could successfully exchange data. Today, all personal computers use ASCII code to represent basic character data.

NOTE

I say "most manufacturers" because IBM chose not to conform to the ASCII standard. To this day, large IBM computers use EBCDIC (Extended Binary Coded Decimal Interchange Code), not ASCII. (This was a typical decision for IBM, who were used to dominating the computer industry before personal computers ran away with it.) And as you'll see towards the end of this chapter, EBCDIC computers continue to cause problems on the Internet.

THE ASCII CHARACTER SET

Inside a computer, data is stored and transmitted as electrical pulses, electronic switches, and magnetic spots. These are essentially *binary* in nature—that is, they can have two states: pulse or no pulse, on or off, positive or negative. So all numeric data must be represented in the binary number system, which has only two digits: 0 and 1. The count from zero to ten in binary numbers goes this way: 0, 1, 10, 11, 100, 101, 110, 111, 1000, 1001, 1010. Each digit is called a *bit*, which stands for *b*inary dig*it*.

The primary unit of data in a computer is the *byte*, which comprises eight bits. So a byte can hold the binary values from 00000000 to 11111111. Translated into our normal decimal number system, that's 0 to 255, or 256 values.

The ASCII code, however, uses only seven of the eight bits. The eighth bit, which is the bit on the left, is reserved for other purposes. So ASCII uses only the values 00000000 to 01111111, or 0 to 127 (128 values in all).

As you can see in Table 2.1, not all 128 values were assigned to printable characters. The first 32 values and the last value (127) were assigned to signals that controlled the teletypewriter (TTY), the most common user device in those days. For example, a 4 indicated the end of text; 7 rang the TTY's bell; 10 moved down a line (without returning the carriage); and 13 returned the carriage to the beginning of the line. Most of these signals are now meaningless, and some systems use the values for extra characters; but the ASCII standard still defines the control signals for these values.

NOTE   ASCII 10 and 13 are still used to indicate a new line on most systems. However, some systems use 10 alone; some use 13 alone; and some (including DOS computers) use 13 followed by 10.

Table 2.1 ASCII Code

Dec	Binary	Char	Dec	Binary	Char
0	00000000	control	64	01000000	@
1	00000001	control	65	01000001	A
2	00000010	control	66	01000010	B
3	00000011	control	67	01000011	C
4	00000100	control	68	01000100	D
5	00000101	control	69	01000101	E
6	00000110	control	70	01000110	F
7	00000111	control	71	01000111	G
8	00001000	control	72	01001000	H
9	00001001	control	73	01001001	I
10	00001010	control (LF)	74	01001010	J
11	00001011	control	75	01001011	K
12	00001100	control	76	01001100	L
13	00001101	control (CR)	77	01001101	M
14	00001110	control	78	01001110	N
15	00001111	control	79	01001111	O
16	00010000	control	80	01010000	P
17	00010001	control	81	01010001	Q
18	00010010	control	82	01010010	R
19	00010011	control	83	01010011	S

Dec	Binary	Char	Dec	Binary	Char
20	00010100	control	84	01010100	T
21	00010101	control	85	01010101	U
22	00010110	control	86	01010110	V
23	00010111	control	87	01010111	W
24	00011000	control	88	01011000	X
25	00011001	control	89	01011001	Y
26	00011010	control	90	01011010	Z
27	00011011	control	91	01011011	[
28	00011100	control	92	01011100	|
29	00011101	control	93	01011101	]
30	00011110	control	94	01011110	^
31	00011111	control	95	01011111	_
32	00100000	space	96	01100000	`
33	00100001	!	97	01100001	a
34	00100010	"	98	01100010	b
35	00100011	#	99	01100011	c
36	00100100	$	100	01100100	d
37	00100101	%	101	01100101	e
38	00100110	&	102	01100110	f
39	00100111	'	103	01100111	g
40	00101000	(	104	01101000	h
41	00101001	)	105	01101001	i
42	00101010	*	106	01101010	j
43	00101011	+	107	01101011	k
44	00101100	,	108	01101100	l
45	00101101	-	109	01101101	m
46	00101110	.	110	01101110	n
47	00101111	/	111	01101111	o
48	00110000	0	112	01110000	p
49	00110001	1	113	01110001	q
50	00110010	2	114	01110010	r
51	00110011	3	115	01110011	s
52	00110100	4	116	01110100	t
53	00110101	5	117	01110101	u

Table 2.1 ASCII Code (continued)

Dec	Binary	Char	Dec	Binary	Char
54	00110110	6	118	01110110	v
55	00110111	7	119	01110111	w
56	00111000	8	120	01111000	x
57	00111001	9	121	01111001	y
58	00111010	:	122	01111010	z
59	00111011	;	123	01111011	{
60	00111100	<	124	01111100	|
61	00111101	=	125	01111101	}
62	00111110	>	126	01111110	~
63	00111111	?	127	01111111	control

By the way, notice that the ASCII characters are the same characters that you'll find on the standard American keyboard. ASCII came first, and it made sense to design keyboards so that you could type all the ASCII characters. We won't talk about other languages, where different characters are needed. That's the subject for another book.

BINARY DATA

Technically, all data is binary data, but we loosely use the term *binary* to mean "not ASCII." To put it another way, binary data has a 1 in the eighth bit. Any file that contains even one byte that is not ASCII is considered to be a binary file and can't be transmitted via Internet email. This includes programs, graphics, spreadsheets, sound waves, video clips, and word processing documents.

Wait a minute—word processing documents? Don't they contain just text? No, most word processing documents also contain a great deal of formatting information: fonts, margin and tab settings, spacing information, bold, italics, and so on. Many also include non-ASCII characters such as *à* and *ô*. (These international characters are called *extended characters* because they're not part of the ASCII character set.) And today, word processing documents might also contain embedded binary information such as spreadsheet ranges, graphics, and the like.

All this extra information has to be expressed using values from 128 to 255, the only values available, and as Shakespeare said, there's the rub. When you use any code above 127, you use the eighth bit, and the file becomes a binary file.

NOTE Two types of word processing files are ASCII files. Files saved as text files—also called plain text, ASCII, ASCII text, DOS text, or Windows text—contain only ASCII characters. Such files usually have the extension **.txt**. In addition, the rich text file (extension **.rtf**) type was specifically designed to permit a certain amount of formatting information in an ASCII file. Almost all modern word processors can save their documents as text or rich text files in addition to the standard word processing types.

THE NEED FOR ENCODING

Way back in ancient times—before 1980—when the Internet was first starting to appear, its primary purpose was to transmit ASCII text messages via email and newsgroups among a few university and government computers. No one foresaw how the Internet would spread throughout the world, connecting government agencies, the military, schools, businesses from international megaconglomerates to SOHOs, and ordinary individuals. It just goes to show that if your product or service fills the right need at the right time, it will sell by word of mouth. There were no formal ads promoting the Internet until recently, but it spread like wildfire.

Nor did anyone foresee how the small, relatively simple applications of those days would mushroom into word processors, spreadsheets, databases, calculators, animation studios, sound studios, graphic designers, recipe analyzers, video and role-playing games, online services... somebody stop me!

And so the early designers decided to use values above 127 as control signals—signals that manage the flow of data. But that means that any data transmitted via Internet email or stored in Usenet newsgroups must not use the eighth bit, or they might accidentally send control signals, creating total chaos. As I said at the outset, all email shipped via the Internet and all data stored in Usenet newsgroups must be ASCII data.

Internet email and Usenet wouldn't be much use if we couldn't transmit spreadsheets, graphics, sound waves, word processing files, and other binary files. We get around the ASCII restriction by encoding binary data as ASCII data long enough to transmit it. We decode it again at the receiving end.

Do you need to encode? That depends entirely on your Internet service provider and your email handler. Online services like AOL automatically encode email for you, using either MIME or a program like uuencode. But if you're using a more basic email handler, you might need to do your own encoding. Even if your service automatically encodes, you will probably have to decode files that you receive via Internet email occasionally. And if you want to download files from Usenet, you will probably have to decode them yourself.

ENCODING WITH UUENCODE

Two early and very popular encoding and decoding programs are known as uuencode and uudecode. (These are pronounced *you-you-encode* and *you-you-decode*.) We'll look at how these programs work in this section.

NOTE   The names uuencode and uudecode tell you a lot about their origins. The Internet originally connected university and government computers running the UNIX operating system. Because data was being transmitted from one UNIX system to another, some of the early Internet program names began with *uu* for *UNIX-to-UNIX*. UNIX is a case-sensitive operating system, unlike DOS or Windows, and UNIX users tend to name their directories, files, and programs using all lowercase—hence, uuencode and uudecode rather than UUEncode and UUDecode.

uuencode converts data three bytes at a time. Let's look at a typical example. Suppose that the first three bytes of a file contain these values, shown in binary:

```
10001000 01010101 11111111
```

The first thing uuencode does is split the 24 bits into four six-bit groups, like this:

```
100010 000101 010111 111111
```

It then inserts leading zeros in front of each group to create four bytes:

```
00100010 00000101 00010111 00111111
```

Now it adds 32 to each byte to make sure that it does not fall into the ASCII no man's land:

```
01000010 00100101 00110111 01011111
```

The four bytes now contain legitimate ASCII values between 32 and 95. Table 2.1 shows that the four encoded bytes represent these characters: B % 7 _. This looks like meaningless data, and it is, but uudecode can easily restore the original values by reversing the encoding process.

A file encoded by uuencode usually has the extension **.uue** or **.uu,** although that's not a requirement. Its contents look something like Figure 2.1. On the first line is the word *begin*, a code indicating read/write permission for UNIX systems (666 in the example), and the name that should be assigned to the file when it is decoded (**time.txt** in the example). This is followed by a blank line.

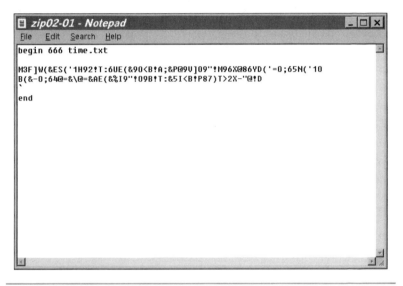

Figure 2.1 *Peeking inside a file encoded by uuencode.*

Each of the text lines starts with a one-byte code, followed by 60 ASCII characters. Some encoders place an extra character at the end of each line to circumvent certain mail handlers that strip trailing spaces. Because a space is not really a space in an encoded file, it's important that trailing spaces are not deleted. Hence, the extra character means that no line ends with a space. But the encoder I used to create the file in Figure 2.1 doesn't do that. Instead, it translates all spaces into apostrophes (').

The first byte on each text line tells uudecode the length of that line. For most text lines, an *M* indicates that there are 60 characters on the line. If the last text line is shorter than 60 characters, you'll see a different character there—it's a B in Figure 2.1. After the text lines come a line containing a single space (which my encoder translated into ') and then a blank line. The last line contains the word *end*.

NOTE   The original file for Figure 2.1 was an uncompressed text file containing this message: Now is the time for all good men and women to come to the aid of their party.

Notice that the original file contained only 76 characters, but uuencode expanded this to 137 characters, including the header and footer lines. Your file does get bigger when you encode it. And unfortunately, you can't compress it after you encode it, because the compression would turn it into a binary file again. So if you're going to both compress and encode, you have to compress first and live with the larger file created by the encoder.

SPLIT FILES

There is a lot of traffic on the Internet, so many servers limit file size. If you receive an encoded file that doesn't contain both the *begin* and the *end* line, you've received one part of a split file. You'll have to locate the rest of the file and bring the parts together before you can decode them.

Where will the rest of the file be? If the file was included in email, the rest of it should be waiting in your mailbox for you—the person who split them would probably make sure to send you all the parts. If the file is in a newsgroup, look for the rest of it on the same board, probably labeled 1/3, 2/3, and so on.

T I P   Some of the more sophisticated Usenet readers, such as America Online's FileGrabber, automatically recognize split files, retrieve all the parts, and concatenate and decode them for you.

PROBLEMS WITH UUENCODE

Unfortunately, uuencode is not a perfect solution to the ASCII/binary problem. A uuencoded file might not pass undamaged through all Internet gateways. So many different types of computers and so many different email handler programs make up the Internet that it's impossible to predict which ones your email will be shunted through as it works its way to its ultimate destination. Some of the main problems are:

- As mentioned before, some email handlers try to save time and space by stripping "unnecessary" trailing spaces from the ends of text lines. But in an encoded file, a trailing space is not really a trailing space but a code for some other value. So some data is lost or scrambled by these mail handlers.

- Some gateways use IBM mainframes, which must translate ASCII code into EBCDIC code to pass through the gateway and then translate it back again. Unfortunately, EBCDIC code has no equivalent for some of the ASCII symbols, so they get lost in the translation. The result? Missing or scrambled data when the file is decoded.

- Some versions of uuencode try to counteract these problems by means such as adding an extra character to the end of each line, translating spaces into apostrophes, translating the characters that EBCDIC trashes into other characters, and so on. But the decoder at the other end might not be aware of these "tricks" and might not be able to decode them properly.

ENTER XXENCODE

These problems are disappearing as older gateways are replaced with newer ones that are more careful to preserve the data. But some of the older ones are still out there. So a program called *xxencode* (and its cousin, *xxdecode*) was developed. It works much like uuencode but avoids the problems of trailing spaces and non-EBCDIC characters. If you encounter a file with the extension **.xx** or **.xxe**, it was probably encoded by xxencode, and you can decode it with xxdecode.

Several of the programs on the disk accompanying this book can encode and decode in uuencode and xxencode format.

T I P

WHAT'S NEXT?

Encoding with uuencode and xxencode is slowly disappearing, being replaced by a much more comprehensive system called MIME. It's more likely that you'll have to deal with MIME-encoded files, at least for your email. Chapter 3 explains how MIME works.

CHAPTER 3

MIME Encoding

You saw in Chapter 2 the old way of encoding email by using uuencode or its cousin xxencode. But most people don't need to manually encode or decode email anymore; their mailers do it for them automatically. It's all done with the subject of this chapter—MIME. I'll even go out on a limb and bet that most people sending email on the Internet today never heard of encoding. (That's a safe bet, isn't it? Who could ever figure out whether I was right? If you have statistics to prove me wrong, email me at judinorth@aol.com. I'll send you a free book.)

What you'll learn in this chapter:

- What MIME is
- How it works
- How you get it
- How MIME encodes files
- How it deals with file types
- How it doesn't deal with compressed data

What MIME Is

Multipurpose Internet Mail Extensions (MIME) is a feature built into most mailers today. When you send a file via email, your MIME mailer automatically encodes it. When your recipients receive the file, their MIME mailers automatically decode the file. Neither senders nor receivers are aware of the encoding.

NOTE Notice that MIME pertains only to email. You still need to do your own encoding for files in Usenet. You might also need to do your own Usenet decoding, if your news reader doesn't do it for you.

But there's more! MIME also keeps track of the type of file—.gif image, Excel spreadsheet, .wav sound clip, or whatever—and the mail reader automatically displays (or plays) the file for the recipient, if it can. Let's look at a typical example. My sister using Eudora wants to send me a photograph of her new grandchild. She starts a new letter, types out a message, and attaches the file to it. Then she clicks the **Send** button, and as far as she is concerned, she is finished.

Eudora mailer looks at the attached file's extension, **.jpg**, and adds a note that the attached file is an image file in JPEG format. It encodes the file using a Base64 scheme much like xxencode's. Then it sends the entire letter on its way.

A few minutes later, I receive the letter on AOL. When I open it and read the message, I see that there is a file attached and click the **Download** button. As AOL downloads the file to my hard drive, it decodes the data, reads the type, and calls upon its **.JPEG** viewer to display the file—the photograph of my new great-nephew appears on my screen.

How Do I Get MIME?

MIME is usually built right into Internet mailers, especially those for PCs and Macs. You probably already have it, whether you're using a service such as AOL, WorldNet, or Microsoft Network that has a built-in mailer or an independent mailer such as Eudora.

If you don't have MIME built into your mailer and you receive MIME-encoded email over the Internet, you'll need to get a separate MIME decoder. You can download one from my Web page at http://www.aol.com/jnfbooks or check your own Internet service provider's software library for a good program.

NOTE   If your mailer doesn't include MIME services, you're better off using uuencode to encode files rather than trying to use a separate MIME program to encode. There are too many arcane decisions you have to make with a separate MIME encoder, and if you choose wrong, your recipients might not be able to decode your files. So if you get a MIME decoder that includes encoding facilities, just ignore those facilities and use uuencode or xxencode.

A Typical MIME-Encoded File

You might occasionally see the contents of a MIME-encoded file, so you might like to know what it looks like. Figure 3.1 shows a typical example, where the file contains lots of binary data, such as a .gif file. Only the beginning of the file is shown—there's too much data in a .gif file to show it all.

```
Mime-Version: 1.0
Content-Type: image/gif; name="55-av.gif"
Content-Transfer-Encoding: base64
Content-Disposition: inline; filename="55-av.gif"

R01GODlhMABAAPcAAAAAADkAAAgIAGspAIwpAIwxAJxKALVSAFIACD
kICFIICGsICIwICCEY
CFIYCGsYCIwYCAgpCDkpCFIpCJQpCGsxCIQxCJwxCABCCJxKCLVKCM
5aCLVjCLUxEGtCEIRK
EOdjELWEEAgAGFIIGGsQGIwQGCkYGIwpGFIxGGsxGIQxGJwxGCFCGF
JCGJxKGLVKGM5SGCla
GJxaGLVjGM5rGJxzGGtKIYRKIZxKIbVSIZxaIWtjIYRrIb2EId6MIS
kpKWsxKZQxKc5SKd5j
```

*Figure 3.1 A typical MIME-encoded file includes headers
and Base64-encoded data.*

The encoded file starts off with several header lines. The ones
in Figure 3.1 are required for all MIME-encoded files, but
most MIME programs insert other headers too. You'll always
see these three headers:

- **MIME-Version** lets the MIME decoder know which
  version of MIME was used to encode the file.

As I write this, version 1.0 is the latest version of MIME.

NOTE

- **Content-Type** documents the type of file so that the mail
  reader knows how to display or play it after decoding.
- **Content-Transfer-Encoding** documents the encoding scheme
  used. We'll talk about the encoding schemes shortly.

The body of the file is the encoded data. It uses somewhat different conventions from uuencode or xxencode. It does not, for example, start each line with a character indicating the length of the line. It does not use *begin* and *end* to mark the boundaries of the data. And, as you'll see shortly, it uses an encoding scheme that selects characters that don't get trashed as they travel the Internet.

HOW MIME ENCODES DATA

MIME uses three encoding methods: 7-bit, quoted-printable, and Base64. Seven-bit is used with all ASCII data. Quoted-printable is more appropriate for files that contain mostly ASCII text with just a few binary characters. Base64 is used for files that contain a lot of binary data, such as images and videos. Let's take a look at each of these methods in a little more detail.

NOTE MIME uses two more types of encoding—8-bit and binary—in situations where the file does not need to be converted to ASCII characters.

7-BIT ENCODING

Actually, that's a misnomer—or is it an oxymoron? The 7-bit method means that the data is not encoded because it is all ASCII data. Why take the time to encode data—and increase the file size—when it doesn't need to be encoded?

QUOTED-PRINTABLE ENCODING

When just a few 8-bit characters are in a file, as in a text file that occasionally uses a bullet or the letter *W*, the quoted-printable method provides the best results. The ASCII characters are left alone. The 8-bit extended characters are encoded as =nn, where *nn* is a two-character code, such as =F1 for *ñ* and =86 for *†*. So the word *piñata* would be encoded this way:

```
pi=F1ata
```

As you can see, the quoted-printable method expanded this word from six characters to eight. Base64 encoding would also produce eight characters, so quoted-printable doesn't save any space on this single word. But consider an entire sentence:

The kids worked for ten minutes to break the piñata! With quoted-printable encoding, the sentence would take only 54 characters, whereas base64 encoding would produce 69 characters. So you can see the advantage of quoted-printable encoding when only a few binary values are involved. However, for data that is mostly binary, as in an image file, the quoted-printable method would nearly triple the size of the file instead of increasing it by a mere third.

MIME's Base64 Encoding

MIME's Base64 encoding is designed to avoid the problems of uuencode. It starts off the same way, by dividing three bytes into four 6-bit groups and inserting leading zeros to create four bytes. But then it alters the new bytes to represent the characters 0–9, a–z, A–Z, +, and /. The result still looks like nonsense (or a cryptogram), but instead of containing a lot of punctuation characters, it contains characters that ride the Internet with no problems.

NOTE

Base64 encoding is the most common form of encoding in MIME. Many of the MIME encoders I have seen choose Base64 encoding, all the time, even for plain ASCII text.

DISPLAYING FILES

A MIME mail reader's capability to display files provides one of the key advantages over earlier forms of encoding. Before MIME, you had to figure out what type of file you received and start the appropriate software to display it, assuming that you had the right software. You also had to find where you downloaded the file on your hard drive—a task that alone defeated many people. (Of course, you still have to find the file if you want to see or hear it a second time.) MIME does away with some of that hassle.

I say "some" intentionally, because your MIME reader probably can't handle every possible file type. The MIME standards require a reader to display ASCII text. Beyond that, it's up to a reader's creators to decide what types of files it will handle. Many readers can display the "standard" file types: text, rich text, .gif images, .jpg images, and .wav sound clips. Beyond that, you're on your own. Some very popular readers, such as Eudora Light, don't do even that much; as of this writing, Eudora Light displays only text files.

NOTE

What happens when your reader doesn't display the file you have just received? You must display it yourself using whatever software you have for that purpose. Suppose, for example, that you have just received a MIDI music clip as an **.mid** file. And suppose that you have Windows 95's Media Player installed. You would start up Media Player, locate and open the **.mid** file that you just downloaded, and listen to the music.

But what if you don't have a MIDI player? You would have to get one before you can listen to the **.mid** file. You can probably download one from somewhere—perhaps from the Internet, your online service, or your BBS.

THE MIME CONTENT TYPES

The Content-Type header is the key to identifying the type of the attached file. It identifies a general type such as "image," a subtype such as "gif," and perhaps some parameters that further define the file, such as "name='55-av.gif'." The allowable parameters depend on the type and subtype.

Table 3.1 lists the major types that all MIME mailers must recognize. There are too many subtypes to list here. More types and subtypes are being proposed all the time, so the next MIME version might include many more.

Table 3.1 MIME Content Types

Type	Interpretation
Text	Text that is readable by humans, containing only ASCII characters; subtypes include plain and enriched.
Image	A photograph, drawing, or other type of graphical image (but not animated); subtypes include gif, jpeg, and tiff.
Audio	Sound; subtypes include basic, wave, and midi.
Video	A moving image; subtypes include mpeg and QuickTime.
Application	Data specific to a particular application, such as an MS Word document or an Excel spreadsheet.

A mailer can make up its own types and subtypes, but it must start their names with x-, as in x-compressed/x-zip. Of course, there's no sense in a mailer doing this unless it knows that the receiving mailer can recognize and handle the type.

N O T E

Your MIME mailer identifies a file's type and subtype by its filename extension. (So that's how the word *extensions* got into Multipurpose Internet Mail Extensions!) If the file's name is **worksched.txt,** for example, a MIME mailer would identify it as text/plain. If the file's name is **photo1.jpg,** it should be identified as image/jpeg. When MIME can't identify the type, it encodes the file as application/octet-stream, the catch-all category.

MULTIPART MESSAGES

Some messages include more than one type of data. For example, suppose that you send a Microsoft Word document that includes an embedded sound clip. MIME includes a *multipart* content type for such messages. When a message is coded as multipart, each part receives its own header. The parts of the message are separated by boundaries.

Some MIME encoders automatically identify all files as multipart.

N O T E

Figure 3.2 shows an example of a multipart message, with the encoded data removed so that you can just see the headers and boundaries. Notice that the first header merely says that the message has multiple parts and identifies the name of the boundary: bbb. Each of the other headers identifies a specific part of the message.

```
Mime-Version: 1.0
Content-Type: multipart/mixed; boundary="bbb"

This message has been encoded by MIME. It must be
decoded
by a MIME decoder before you can see (or hear)
the enclosed data.

--bbb
Content-Type: image/gif; name="55-av.gif"
Content-Transfer-Encoding: base64

[encoded data goes here]

--bbb
Content-Type: audio/basic; name="greetings.wav"
Content-Transfer-Encoding: base64

[encoded data goes here]

--bbb--
```

Figure 3.1 *A multipart message contains several different messages separated by boundaries.*

Before the first boundary, there is a message that is ignored by MIME decoders—the recipient never sees it; this message has been encoded by MIME, etc. But if the letter is received by a mailer that doesn't include MIME, the recipient will see the message and get some kind of clue how to decode the "secret message" he or she has just received.

After that message comes the first boundary, with two hyphens before the *bbb* Then comes the first encoded file, a gif file named **55-av.gif**. Then comes another boundary and the second encoded file, a wav file called **greetings.wav**. Because that is the last file in the letter, it is followed by the final boundary, which has hyphens before and after the *bbb*.

MIME and Compressed Files

Have you noticed that *compressed* is not one of the MIME content types? There are no zip, arc, or arj subtypes. So what happens when you send a zipped file from a MIME mailer? It encodes the file in Base64, probably identifying it as application/octet-stream.

The MIME mail reader at the receiving end may or may not know how to unzip the file. I don't know of any current mail reader that will decode, unzip, and then display the file—but I'll bet those facilities are coming in the near future.

What's Next?

You're ready to start decompressing and decoding files... but where do you get the files? As you'll learn in the next section, someone could email them to you. Or you could download them from a Web page or from your local BBS or the Internet. You'll also learn how to send files to other people by emailing or uploading them.

PART II

Uploading and Downloading Files

Chapter 4

Exchanging Files in Email

You want to send a spreadsheet via email to a colleague in Germany—how do you do it? And after she makes changes and emails it back, how do you download it from your email service? That's what this chapter is about—not just spreadsheets, but any kind of file that you want to exchange with others via email.

What you'll learn in this chapter:

- When you need to attach a file and when you don't
- How to attach a file, zipped or unzipped, with and without MIME
- How to receive an attached file, zipped or unzipped, with and without MIME
- How to attach a file using America Online's mailer
- How to download a file using America Online's mailer
- How to attach a file using Eudora Light
- How to download a file using Eudora Light

I chose America Online and Eudora Light because these are two of the most widely used mailers, and they represent two different approaches to attaching and downloading attached files. If you use a different mailer, perhaps the one that's built into your company's network, the examples here should help you figure out how to use yours.

ATTACHING FILES TO EMAIL

If all you want to do is send a fairly short text message to a friend, you don't need to send a file. Just type the text in the body of the letter and send it on its way. It can travel the Internet without needing to be compressed or encoded, and your friend can answer you the same way.

But if you want to send any kind of binary data or any information in a separate file, you must *attach* the file to the letter. Your letter arrives at its destination with a note that a file is attached. Your friend downloads the attached file to his or her hard drive. A MIME reader may interpret the file as it downloads.

Here's the usual procedure for attaching a file:

1. Archive and compress the file(s) to be sent, producing a single file.
2. Encode the file (unless you have a MIME mailer).
3. Write a text message to accompany the file.
4. Attach the file to the letter.
5. Send the letter. The attached file is automatically uploaded.

If you receive such a letter, here's what you would usually do:

1. Read the message.
2. Download the file.
3. Decode the file, if it's encoded.
4. Unzip the file.
5. Scan for viruses.
6. Do whatever is necessary to view or process the file.

If the last step sounds vague, it can't be helped. How you process a file depends on what it is. If it's a piece of software, for example, you might install it and run it. If it's a word processing document, you would open it in your word processor. If it's a spreadsheet, you would open it in your spreadsheet program, and so on.

So far, we've been assuming that the attached file is zipped. But if the file is already compressed—for example, if it's a .gif or .jpeg image, a video clip, or a sound clip—it doesn't need to be zipped unless you want to archive several files together. You also might decide not to zip a file if it's short. Or if you know that your recipient wouldn't have a frog's notion how to unzip a file.

If you have a MIME mailer, it becomes even easier to send the file because you don't need to bother with encoding. It's also much easier to download a file with MIME because it is not only decoded automatically, but your mailer also might interpret it.

Now let's look at how to deal with attached files in a couple of popular mailers.

ATTACHED FILES IN AMERICA ONLINE

America Online's mailer includes MIME, so you don't need to encode the files that you attach. But if you want to zip them, you have to do that using a separate program such as PKZip or WinZip. When the file is ready (zipped or not), here's how to attach it, using WAOL 3.0:

1. Click the **Compose Mail** icon to open a blank letter, as shown below.

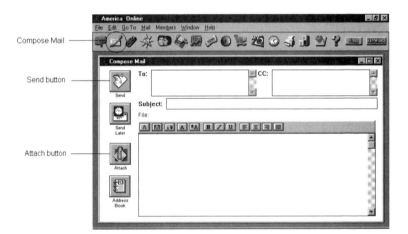

2. Fill out the address and subject and write a note to accompany the file.

AOL won't send a letter when the body is blank.

NOTE

3. Click the **Attach** button. AOL opens a browse dialog box where you can locate and select the file to be attached.

4. Select the file and click **Open**. AOL attaches the file to the letter, as shown below.

5. Click **Send** to send the file.

Now suppose that you receive an attached file. You'll see several clues that a file is attached. First, you'll see an attached file icon 📎 rather than a solo letter icon 📄 in your mail list. Also, the letter itself will look something like Figure 4.1, where you can see the name of the attached file as well as **Download** buttons.

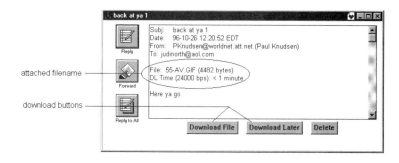

Figure 4.1 *You see several clues that a file is attached to a letter in AOL*

If you click the **Download File** button, AOL pops up a browse box where you can rename the file and select a directory for it. Then AOL decodes and downloads the file into the selected directory and interprets it if possible.

T I P

AOL might even unzip a file for you, depending on your download preferences (see keyword **MY AOL**). But it won't unzip the file until you sign off, and it won't go on to interpret a file after unzipping it.

If you click the **Download Later** button, AOL adds the file to your Download Manager list. Download Manager is a complex subject that's capable of reducing grown men and women to tears. I hate to brush over it lightly, but I simply don't have the room to cover it here. Here are a few notes to help you get started:

- When you try to sign off, Download Manager interrupts to ask whether you want to download files now. If you say yes, all the files on your Download Manager list are downloaded. Then you are signed off automatically.

- The files being downloaded receive their default names and go into the default download directory, which is probably aol30\download, unless you (or someone else) changed it.

- Download Manager does not interpret files. You must find them on your hard disk and view, play, or otherwise process them yourself.

- Choose **File|Download Manager** for information about the files that have been downloaded or are waiting to be downloaded.

Attached Files in Eudora Light

Eudora Light gives you a choice of using MIME or BinHex. You would choose MIME for your PC, as shown in Figure 4.2. You also can enable or disable quoted-printable mode. When it's enabled, appropriate attachments are encoded using the quoted-printable method; otherwise, they are all encoded using Base64. Quoted-printable is enabled in Figure 4.2.

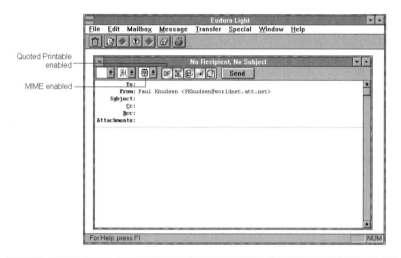

Figure 4.2 Eudora Light gives you the option of using MIME and quoted-printable.

Assuming that MIME is selected, here is how you would attach a file to a letter using Eudora Light:

1. Click the **New Message** icon to open a blank letter, as shown in Figure 4.2.

2. Fill out the address and subject and write a note to accompany the file.

3. Choose **Message|Attach File**. Eudora Light opens a browse dialog where you can locate and select the file to be attached.

4. Select the file and click **OK**. Eudora Light attaches the file to the letter, as shown below.

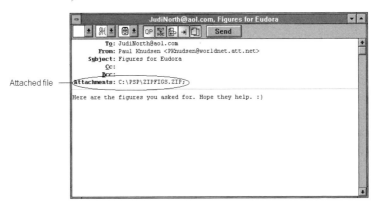

Attached file

5. Click **Send** to send the file.

You have to be online to send the file. Everything else can be done offline.

NOTE

You don't have to do anything special to download an attached file in Eudora Light. As soon as you receive a letter, any attached file is automatically decoded and downloaded into your default download directory. You'll see a progress window while the file is downloading. You can find out what the file is and where it was downloaded by reading the message it was attached to, as shown in Figure 4.3.

T I P

You can change the default download directory by choosing **SpeciallSettings**. Then select the **Attachments** category.

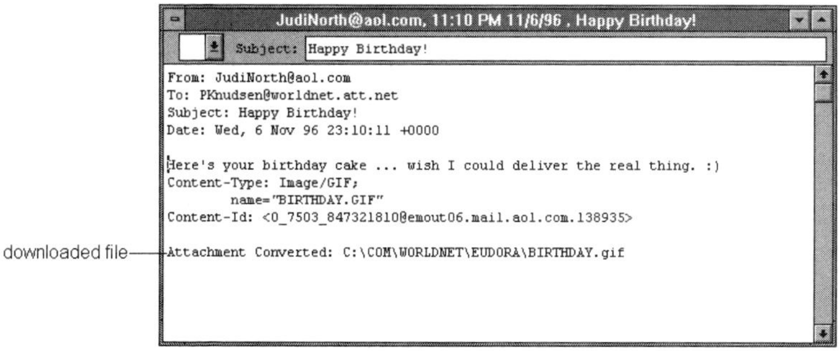

JudiNorth@aol.com, 11:10 PM 11/6/96 , Happy Birthday!

Subject: Happy Birthday!

From: JudiNorth@aol.com
To: PKnudsen@worldnet.att.net
Subject: Happy Birthday!
Date: Wed, 6 Nov 96 23:10:11 +0000

Here's your birthday cake ... wish I could deliver the real thing. :)
Content-Type: Image/GIF;
        name="BIRTHDAY.GIF"
Content-Id: <0_7503_847321810@emout06.mail.aol.com.138935>

downloaded file————Attachment Converted: C:\COM\WORLDNET\EUDORA\BIRTHDAY.gif

---

Figure 4.3 *Eudora Light identifies a downloaded file in the body of the message.*

WHAT'S NEXT?

Sometimes you have to go out and seek the files you want to download. One place to find thousands of files is on the World Wide Web. The next chapter shows you how to download files from the Web.

CHAPTER 5

Downloading Files from the World Wide Web

No one knows how many sites are available on the World Wide Web, but it probably numbers in the hundreds of thousands. And many of them offer files for you to download: software, cursors, photos, works of art, video clips—perhaps millions of downloadable files. But even at sites that don't actually *offer* files, you can usually pull image and sound files from the page if you know how. That's what this chapter is about.

What you'll learn in this chapter:

- A bit of background on the Web (especially Web terminology)
- How to download files that you are intended to download
- How to download files not intended for download
- How to find the files that you have downloaded
- How to use the files that you have downloaded

This chapter necessarily deals with *Web browsers*—those programs that let you visit, see, and hear Web sites. We'll concentrate on the three most popular Web browsers: Netscape 3.0, Internet Explorer 3.0, and America Online's Web browser for Windows 3.*x*.

A BRIEF WEB PRIMER

The process is fascinating—no, it's beyond fascinating—it's downright mesmerizing. You can start off with an advertisement for sportfishing in the Florida Keys, link to the Florida Keys chamber of commerce, from there to Key West, and then to the Hemingway House. And that reminds you that you've been meaning to read some Hemingway, so you find a Hemingway site (shown in Figure 5.1), read his biography, download a couple of photos, print a list of his novels and short stories, and listen to Charleton Heston reading "The Snows of Kilamanjaro" (**http://town.hall.org/Archives/radio/IMS/HarperAudio/012494_harp_ITH.html**).

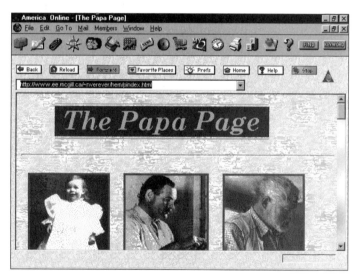

Figure 5.1 *The Papa Page is at*
http://www.ee.mcgill.ca/~nverever/hem/pindex.html.

Then you link to a page about Heston, which leads you to the Screen Actors Guild, then to a movie trivia contest, and a list of

Academy Award nominees. That reminds you of a movie you want to see tonight, so you look up movies in your area (shown in Figure 5.2) and find out when and where it's playing.

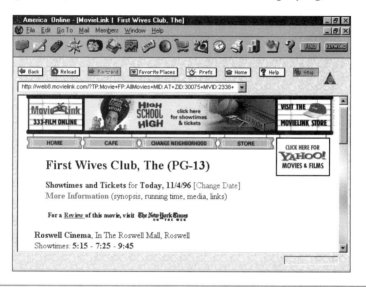

Figure 5.2 MovieLink is located at http://www.777film.com.

In a couple of hours, you have traveled from the Florida Keys to your local UA8 by way of Paris, Pamplona, Mount Kilamanjaro, and Hollywood. You have linked to nearly 20 different computers in four countries on two continents without knowing it, because all you did was click items that looked interesting to you. That's the Web.

WHAT IS THE WEB?

Its formal name is the World Wide Web, and it used to be abbreviated as WWW; but today most people just call it *the Web*. It's made up of sites all over the world, from extremely professional sites, such as Microsoft's, to rank amateur, often fascinating, sites created by individuals like you and me who just want to say hello to the world and talk about their favorite pastimes. The majority of sites fall somewhere in between. You probably can't think of a topic that isn't covered somewhere on the Web. (Please don't send me a list of topics that you couldn't find on the Web. Just because you can't find a topic doesn't mean it's not there.)

Large and small businesses, political campaigns, unions, churches, grade school classes, newspapers, radio and TV stations, museums, publishers, authors—everyone wants to have a web site. I have three of them, one for my friends and family, one for a group that I belong to, and one for you, Dear Reader.

A Web site is made up of one or more *pages*. Each page is a Web document that might contain text, images, links to other pages, audio, animation, and other elements. Usually, one page per site is considered the *home page*, serving to introduce the site and index and link to the other pages. The other pages usually link back to the home page, perhaps to each other, and often to other sites as well.

NOTE Potentially, you can get from one Web site to any other Web site in the world just by following links. (Some sites are dead ends, but you can always back up and take another path.) If you envision all those links as lines, you'll see why they call it the World Wide Web.

THE WEB AND THE INTERNET

The Internet makes the Web possible. Each Web site is located on a computer that is part of the Internet, running special *Web server* software to give you access to its Web sites. You must have some kind of connection to the Internet to access Web sites. You also have to have a Web browser, as mentioned at the beginning of this chapter.

When you go out exploring on the Web, searching for information and linking from page to page and site to site, you are said to be *Web browsing*. If you're just free-floating, clicking whatever links strike your fancy without looking for anything in particular, you are *surfing the Web*. I have often started after something specific and ending up surfing. Sigh.

T I P

We should stop for a moment to pay tribute to the first popular Web browser, the one that helped the Web start its phenomenal growth, Mosaic. For a while, everyone was talking about Mosaic, but it has been surpassed by Netscape, Internet Explorer, and AOL's web browser in the past couple of years. Internet Explorer is based on Mosaic, however.

N O T E

Like all Internet resources, Web pages are accessed by their *Universal Resource Locators* (URLs), which are often referred to simply as their addresses. The URL for a Web page starts with **http://** followed by the name of the Web server. The Web server is usually, but not always, followed by a single slash and the pathname of the page. (If the pathname is omitted, the default of **index.html** is assumed.) For example, Microsoft's home page is at **http://microsoft.com**. My home page is at **http://members.aol.com/jnfbooks**. I have another homepage at **http://members.aol.com/judinorth**.

The expression *http* stands for the *HyperText Transport Protocol*, the rules that govern Web pages on the Internet.

T I P

It's All Done with HTML

Webmasters (the people who create and maintain Web pages) work their magic with a special language called *HyperText Markup Language* (HTML). It's actually a fairly simple language, in which Web browser commands are enclosed in angle brackets, as in **<BOLD>** for bold face type. Anything

outside angle brackets is displayed on the page as text. A Web
browser interprets the commands to create the Web page. For
example, Figure 5.3 shows the HTML used to create one of my
Web pages. Don't worry if you can't read or understand the
HTML—I just wanted you to see what it looks like.

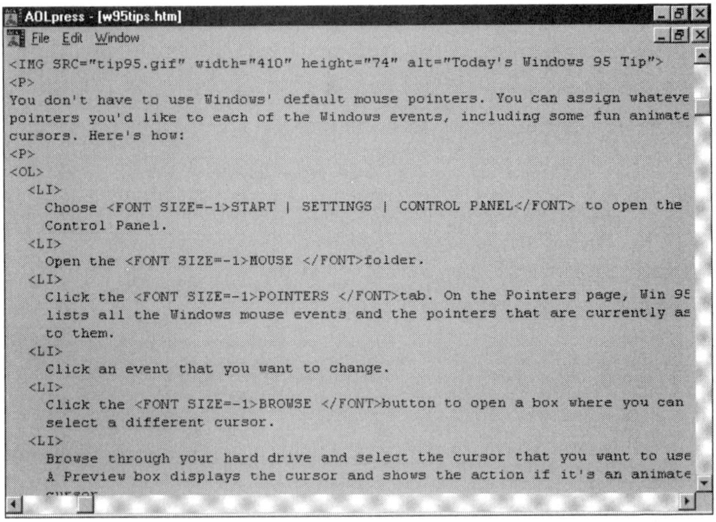

Figure 5.3 *This is part of the HTML that creates the Web page
shown in Figure 5.5, later in this chapter.*

All Web browsers must understand basic HTML. But just like
the Web itself, HTML is growing and changing daily. Many of
the new features have not been standardized yet, so browsers
differ in how they handle them. Unfortunately, this means that
a page might look great on one browser and terrible—even
completely unreadable—on another. Wise Webmasters design
their pages for the lowest common denominator, limiting their
HTML commands to those that every browser understands.
But that takes away some of the fun of exploring the latest
and most exciting techniques, so not every Webmaster can
resist the temptation of a new HTML feature.

How About Some Java?

HTML is all very well and good, but it's kind of static. You can display things, but you can't animate them. And interaction is fairly primitive—you can click a link or fill out a form, but that's about it. To add real spice to a site, you need Java. This programming language from Sun Microsystems lets people create *applets* (small programs) that can be included right on a Web page. Many more interesting things can be done with animation, sound, and interaction, as you'll discover in your surfing expeditions. I have played with all kinds of games, simulations, Web chat rooms, interactive maps, and much more. The applet in Figure 5.4, for example, maps the New York City subway system and calculates a route between any two points that you select.

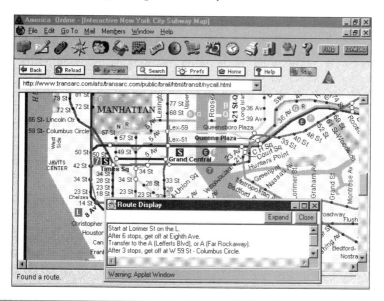

Figure 5.4 This interactive subway map can be found at http://www.transarc.com/afs/transarc.com/public/brail/html/transit/nycall.html.

Check my Web page at **http://members.aol.com/jnfbooks** for links to some fun Java applets.

T I P

Java applets won't work on every Web browser. The browser has to be Java enabled. Of the browsers we'll deal with in this chapter, Netscape 3.0 and Internet Explorer 3.0 are Java enabled. As of this writing, AOL's browser for Windows 3.*x* is not Java enabled, but its browser for Windows 95 (which is really Internet Explorer 3.0 with a different user interface) is.

Java is not the only way to jazz up a page. There are competing programming languages and other ways to animate images. But Java is the most prevalent, and many Web browsers can now handle Java applets.

N O T E

FILES THAT YOU ARE INTENDED TO DOWNLOAD

Take a look at one of my Web pages, shown in Figure 5.5. You can see that I have included a couple of files for people to download. You would download one of the files by clicking the graphic that says **Download Red Horse** or **Download Einstein**. Many pages include similar graphics or just a text link; in either case, a simple click begins the download.

Let's assume that you have found a file that you want to download. Your mouse pointer is poised over the download graphic (or text). Here are the steps you would follow:

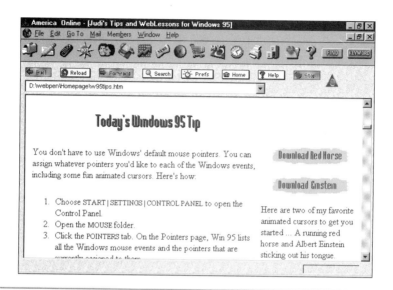

Figure 5.5 *You download a file from this page by clicking one of the two download "buttons."*

1. Click the download graphic or text. In response, your browser probably pops up a common Save As dialog where you can check and change the name of the file and the download directory.

T I P

One of the biggest headaches people give themselves is finding files after they are downloaded. A 1.2G hard drive can become the proverbial haystack when you don't remember the name of the file or where it is stored. If necessary, write down the filename and the directory *before* you click that **OK** button.

2. Click **OK** in the Save As dialog. Your browser might
    display a progress box as it downloads the file.
    Netscape's progress box is shown in Figure 5.6. When
    the progress box disappears, you know the download is
    finished. AOL does not display a separate progress box,
    but the progress is displayed in the status bar (the
    bottom line) of the browser window.

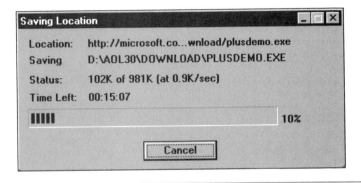

*Figure 5.6 Netscape displays this progress box while
downloading a file.*

3. Sign off, if desired. You don't need to be online for steps 4,
    5, and 6.

4. If the file is zipped or otherwise compressed, use WinZip
    to locate and decompress it. Most Webmasters try to
    shorten your download time (as well as their upload
    time) by compressing the files they offer you. Some will
    be self-extracting files; the majority are simply zipped,
    and you have to unzip them via PKUnzip, WinZip, or a
    similar product.

Files on the Web don't need to be encoded, so you don't have to worry about decoding them.

TIP

5. Virus check your hard drive, just for safety's sake. Every time you download a file from the Web, you are susceptible to downloading a virus with it.

6. Now you can install, view, or listen to your new file(s), depending on what they are.

FILES THAT YOU AREN'T INTENDED TO DOWNLOAD

You might find graphics or sounds on a Web page that you would like to keep on your hard drive so that you can use them offline. You might want to use a painting as your Windows wallpaper, for example, or listen to a recording while you work. You might even want to use them on your own Web page, but you wouldn't do that unless they were in the public domain, of course.

How can you download something from a Web page when there's nothing to click to start the download? Keep in mind that when you link to the Web page, your browser downloads all its objects to your computer's memory; that's why it takes so long to access Web pages that have a lot of graphics or sound. So the information you want to save is already in your computer's memory, and all you have to do is save it, if only you can separate it out from the rest of the page.

WHEN THE FILE STANDS ALONE

Sometimes the Webmaster makes it easy for you by giving you an object on its own page. Works of art and sound clips are often done this way. Let's look at a couple of examples.

Figure 5.7 shows a page from one of the world's most popular Web sites, the WebMuseum (**http://sunsite.unc.edu/wm**—but when you get there, switch to whichever mirror site is closest to you), which exhibits digitized photos of classical paintings from museums all over the world, as well as a growing collection of music. Notice in the figure that several small versions of some paintings are shown. These are known as *thumbnails*, and they serve to graphically index the actual digitized paintings, which are much larger.

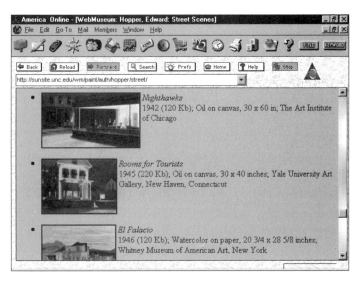

*Figure 5.7 At the WebMuseum, Edward Hopper's paintings
are exhibited first as thumbnails.*

When you find a painting that you want to see on a larger scale, you click its thumbnail to link to the larger version. Figure 5.8 shows what happened when I clicked the *Nighthawks* thumbnail in Figure 5.7. Now I can see the painting in much more detail. Notice in the URL that I am no longer looking at an HTML document but at the actual .jpg graphics file. This often happens when you click a thumbnail graphic. Now that I've got the .jpgfile itself, all I have to do is save it on my hard disk, and the painting is mine. You can do the same with any type of file represented by itself rather than embedded on an HTML page.

Figure 5.8 When you click a thumbnail, you often get a .jpg or .gif file that you can save on your hard drive.

Many sound clips also get their own page instead of being embedded in an HTML document. Figure 5.9 provides another extremely popular example, from the White House site (**http://www.whitehouse.gov**). When you click the button, you hear a recording of Socks, the Clintons' cat. Here again, the file is not embedded in an HTML document. Its URL tells you that it is an AU file. You can add it to your hard drive simply by saving it.

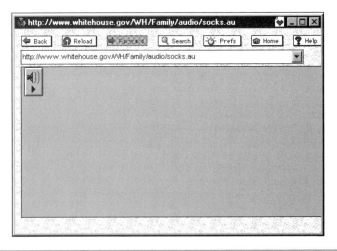

Figure 5.9 It's the cat's meow: Sound clips often come on pages by themselves like this recording of First Cat Socks.

Now the question becomes, how do you save a file when you're Web browsing? The answer depends on your browser. Most browsers have **Save** and **Save As** commands on the **File** menu that work just like they do in other applications. America Online has both commands; Netscape has a **Save As** command; and Internet Explorer has **Save** and **Save As File**.

WHEN THE FILE IS EMBEDDED

What if you would love to download a picture or sound, but there's no link to it as a separate page? If you can see it on a Web page, you can save it on your hard drive; but it takes a little more work—and a generous dose of chutzpah. You're going to peek at the HTML to find the URL of the element that you want.

I'll use one of my own Web pages as an example. In Figure 5.10, you can see four graphical objects: the line at the top of the screen, the **MS Word Tip of the Day** label, the reproduction of Word's zoom control, and the bullets at the bottom.

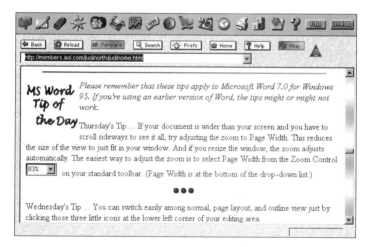

Figure 5.10 My Tips and WebLessons Web page includes several embedded images.

Suppose that you really like that line at the top—it fades from dark to light blue—and you want to use it on your Web page. (Feel free to take it. It's my own creation and you're welcome to it.) Here's how you would do it:

1. Save the Web page on your hard drive. Be sure to notice its filename and directory.

> Some Web browsers let you peek at the HTML without saving the page on your hard drive. For example, with Netscape you would choose View|Document Source, then skip to step 3.

T I P

2. Open the saved Web page as a document in your word processor. You will see the HTML document, with all those HTML commands in angle brackets. Figure 5.11 shows the HTML document for the section of my Web page in Figure 5.10.

> If you have an HTML editor, you might want to use that rather than your word processor.

T I P

3. Find the <IMG> tag for the image that you want. The <IMG> tag is the HTML command to display an image. I have circled the right one in Figure 5.11.

4. The SRC= parameter tells you the name of the file you want to download. In the example in Figure 5.11, it is **bluerule.gif**.

5. In the URL for the Web page, remove anything after the last slash and insert the filename instead. In Figure 5.10, you would remove **judihome.html** and substitute **bluerule.gif**.

The resulting URL would be **http://members.aol.com/ judinorth/bluerule.gif.**

6   Go to that URL, and you should end up with the image file on a page by itself.

7.   Save the file to your hard disk.

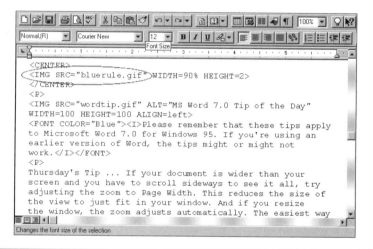

Figure 5.11 *Even if you can't read HTML, you should be able to find the <IMG> tag for the image you want to save.*

Sometimes an <IMG> tag shows a complete URL rather than just the filename. For example, you might see **<IMG SRC="http://members.aol.com/ judinorth/bluerule.gif">**. In that case, just go to that URL to see the image on a separate page.

T I P

After you've saved a bunch of images on your hard drive, how can you see them again? If you don't have an image viewer such as Photoshop or Paintshop, your Web browser can probably be used as a viewer. Look for an **Open** or **Open File** command on the **File** menu; it should let you browse for an image (or sound) file and open it.

You can also take a second look at HTML documents that you have saved this way.

T I P

WHAT'S NEXT?

Millions of files are out there, just waiting for you: shareware, images, sounds, videos, application templates, and documents of all types. They're stored in software libraries, newsgroups, and FTP sites. All you have to do is find them and download them. That's what the next chapter is about.

CHAPTER 6

Downloading from FTP, Gopher, and Usenet

FTP, Gopher, and Usenet use different Internet protocols, but offer similar services: all provide sites where people can upload messages and files for you to read and download. Your online service and your local BBS probably have similar services in the form of forums, bulletin boards, and software libraries. This chapter explains how to use such services, locate files on them, and download those files.

What you'll learn in this chapter:

- A little bit of background and terminology for FTP, Gopher, and Usenet
- How to locate FTP, Gopher, and Usenet sites
- How to download files from each type of site

THE FILE TRANSFER PROTOCOL (FTP)

The File Transfer Protocol (FTP) lets people post files on an Internet computer called an *FTP server*. An FTP site, like the one shown in Figure 6.1 is not very attractive or dynamic—it looks pretty much like a Windows directory list. You open and close the various folders by double-clicking them to find the files that it offers. When you find a file that you want, you click it to download it. Not only is it simpler than the Web, it's also considerably faster because the information it contains is much less complex.

T I P

Unlike the Usenet protocol, FTP permits binary files, so that you don't have to encode and decode binary files.

```
ftp.winsite.com:/pub/pc                                    ▼ _ □ ✕

  ⟳  Connected to ftp.winsite.com

  Uploaded:    Filename:                      Byte Size:
    08/31/96      .message                        159       ▲
  □ 08/31/96      README                          530
    05/02/95      menu                            270
  ▬ 08/31/96      starter                           -
  📁 12/10/96     win3                              -
  📁 12/10/96     win95                             -
  📁 12/05/96     winnt                             -
                                                            ▼

        Open          More        Download        Help
                                    Now
```

Figure 6.1 A typical FTP site includes files grouped into folders.

ANONYMOUS FTP

FTP was originally designed for exchanging files among government agencies and colleges, and it wasn't intended for the general public. So you're supposed to have the proper credentials—a user name and password—to access an FTP site. But as with so many Internet services, FTP grew way beyond its original boundaries—it was too useful to keep private—and most sites are available to all comers. They get around the credential problem by authorizing users named "anonymous." You sign on to the site using the name "anonymous," and all is well. You'll sometimes see yourself referred to as "anonymous" or "anonymous FTP."

To prevent FTP sites from looking like many Usenet sites, anonymous uploading is restricted or forbidden at most FTP sites.

TIP

Every once in a while, you'll be turned away from a site—or certain areas of a site—because it doesn't permit anonymous access. If you really need to access such a site, you must set up a user name and password with the site.

Your local host might use your email address as your password for the anonymous user name.

TIP

ACCESSING FTP

How do you access FTP? You must use a program called an *FTP client*. The client pulls information out of the server and presents it to you. Your online service or BBS might provide an FTP client for you to use. Web browsers also act as FTP clients, so if you can browse the Web, you can access FTP as well. All you have to do is request an FTP URL rather than an http one. To access the White House's FTP site using my Web browser, for example, I go to ftp://ftp.whitehouse.gov.

Web pages can link to FTP sites as well as other Web pages, so you might sometimes link to an ftp site without realizing it until you get there.

T I P

If you don't have an FTP client, or you don't like the snail's pace of your Web browser, you might consider getting a separate client. But you have to run that software "on top" of your Internet access software, which takes a lot of extra knowledge. So unless you're ready to deal with such creatures as Winsock and Telnet, you'll need to get an expert to help you.

ACCESSING FTP FROM AMERICA ONLINE

Many services provide a built-in FTP client—America Online's is typical. The keyword FTP takes you to the FTP area, where you click a **Go to FTP** button. You then see the Anonymous FTP dialog box shown in Figure 6.2. From there, you can select one of the **Favorite Sites** or click the **Other Site** button to go to the Other Site dialog box, also shown in Figure 6.2, where you can enter the address of the site you want. The Other Site dialog box also lets you access sites that don't permit anonymous FTP by entering the correct name and password for the site you want.

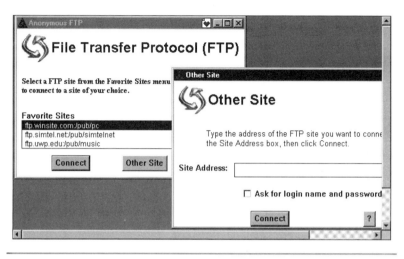

Figure 6.2 *These dialog boxes let you access FTP sites from America Online.*

ACCESSING FTP FROM NETSCAPE NAVIGATOR

When you want to access an FTP site from a Web browser, you turn the FTP address into a URL. Figure 6.3 shows a typical example from Netscape Navigator 3.0. I clicked the **Open** button to get the Open Location dialog box shown near the middle of the figure. I entered the address prefixed by ftp://, as shown in the dialog box. The result was the FTP site you see in the background.

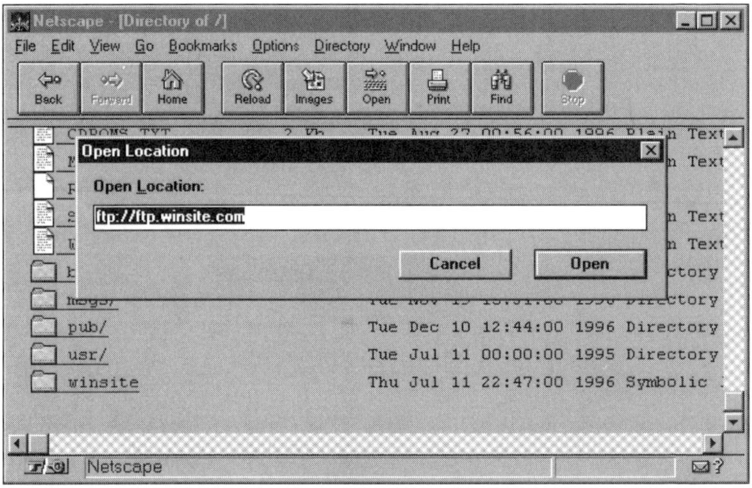

Figure 6.3 *You can access FTP sites from Web browsers such as Netscape Navigator.*

Accessing FTP from FTP Explorer

Figure 6.4 shows how you might access FTP sites via an independent FTP client. The software in the example is FTP Explorer 1.0 for Windows 95 from FTPx Corp., which presents FTP sites using the same interface as Windows 95's Explorer. In the example, I have opened the Quick Connect dialog box and typed the address of the Winsite FTP site, which you can see in the background. You can search your service's software library for FTP clients that provide similar functions, but remember that it takes some extra knowledge to get an independent FTP client up and running.

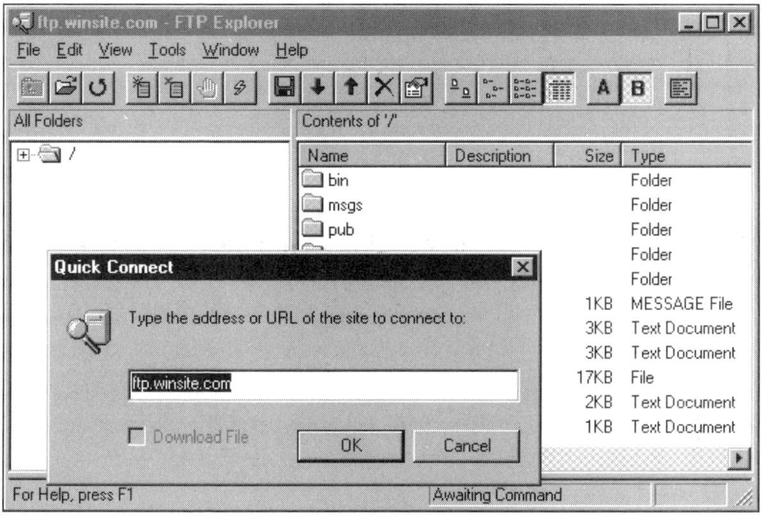

Figure 6.4 *Another way to access FTP is with an independent client such as FTP Explorer.*

You can download FTP Explorer from http://www.ftpx.com.

T I P

LOCATING FTP SITES

FTP comprises tens of thousands of server sites, each offering several million files for you to download. How do you find a specific file among all that information if you don't know what site it's at? The answer is, you have to search for it. Your FTP local host might have a built-in search tool. If not, you can use a handy Internet service called Archie, whose sole purpose is to provide a searchable index to FTP sites.

Let's look at an example. I wanted to download a copy of George Washington's farewell address. I was pretty sure it was available; several universities have made historic documents available via FTP. I tried it first with my FTP client's built-in search tool and then with Archie.

SEARCHING WITH A BUILT-IN SEARCH TOOL

America Online's FTP area has its own search tool, so I started with that. Clicking the **Search** button opened the dialog box shown in Figure 6.5. After several false starts with search phrases like "farewell" and "Washington" (too general), "Washington Farewell Address" (too specific), and "Washington Famous Speeches" (closer, but still no cigar), I finally came up with the phrase shown in the figure, "history and addresses." (It helps to be able to think like an FTP site manager. Obviously, I'm not so good at that.)

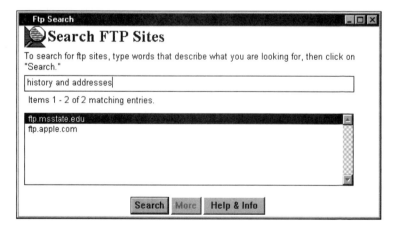

Figure 6.5 *Many services and BBSs provide their own FTP search services; this is America Online's.*

The searcher came up with two sites, and I chose to follow the first one, which turned out to be Mississippi State University. I subsequently opened folders for pubs, history, USA, and early_republic, where I found the farewell address (see Figure 6.6).

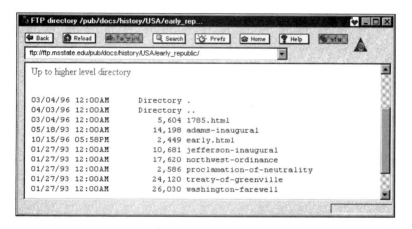

Figure 6.6 *I finally found Washington's farewell address in this folder.*

SEARCHING WITH ARCHIE

Frankly, I wasn't too pleased with AOL's search tool. I didn't think it indexed enough FTP sites, and it took me a long time to find the file I wanted. I decided to try the same search with Archie.

Archie services are provided by several *Archie servers* around the world. Because they don't necessarily keep track of the same sites, you might get different results by contacting different servers. There are several ways to access an Archie server:

- Your FTP server might include a built-in Archie client.
- You can use a separate Archie client.

- You can use Telnet to access an Archie server directly (no client involved).

- You can use email to request information from an Archie server.

Using an Archie Client

An Archie client is a program that you use to access information from an Archie server. It might be built into your FTP client, or you might need a separate program. Figure 6.7 shows a stand-alone Archie client called fpArchie from fpWare. As with separate FTP clients, a separate Archie client runs "on top" of your Internet service provider, and you have to know how to make that happen or get some expert help in setting up your Archie client.

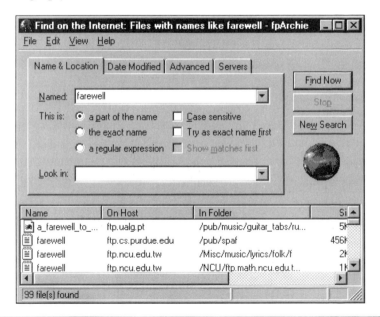

Figure 6.7 You can use fpArchie by itself or call it from FTP Explorer.

To use fpArchie, you simply enter the search phrase in the **Named** box and click **Find Now**. The results are presented in the list box. You can download a file directly from the list box by right-clicking it and choosing **Retrieve** from the resulting context menu. fpArchie acts as the FTP client, accesses the FTP site, and downloads the file. Or, if you want to explore the site to see what else it has to offer, you can copy the document's URL to your Windows Clipboard and then paste it into your Web browser or FTP client. You copy the URL by right-clicking the document and choosing **Copy URL** from the context menu.

Notice the **Servers** tab in the fpArchie window. Clicking that tab opens a list of Archie servers so that you can try your search on a different server, if necessary. (The other tabs are the same as those in Windows 95's Find window.)

FTP Explorer (refer back to Figure 6.4) includes a **Tools|Find** command that is disabled unless you install fpArchie. If FTP Explorer finds fpArchie on your hard disk, the **Tools|Find** command opens its window. fpArchie also can be used independently of FTP Explorer, or any FTP client, however.

Accessing Archie by Email

If you don't have access to Archie online, you can do an Archie search by email. Here's how:

1. Address the email to archie@*server*. For example, if you want to use the Archie server at Rutgers, you would address it to archie@archie.rutgers.edu. Some other possibilities in the United States are:

   archie@archie.internic.net

   archie@archie.unl.edu

archie@archie.sura.net

archie@archie.ans.net

2. In the body of the letter, type this message:

```
set mailto your-email-address
find search phrase
quit
```

For example, I would enter the following lines to locate FTP files with "farewell" in their names:

```
set mailto judinorth@aol.com
find farewell
quit
```

3. Send the mail. You'll receive a response sometime soon.

This procedure uses three Archie commands: set, find, and quit. There are many more commands that you can use to set the parameters for the search. To receive a complete list of commands, send the following letter to the server:

```
set mailto your-email-address
help
quit
```

Accessing an Archie Server by Telnet

Telnet is a service that lets you use your Internet service provider as a link to another server. Many multiuser games (MUGs) are Telnet applications. You sign on with your Internet service provider and then start up the game software, which logs you on to the game server simply by using its Internet address (and usually a port number). This way, you don't have to dial into the game server directly, and your only phone call is to your local Internet number.

To access an Archie server via Telnet, you need a Telnet client such as WinTel 3.1.6 by Satyavrat Mehrotra, shown in Figure 6.8. As with the other clients we've talked about in this chapter, Telnet clients run "on top" of your Internet service provider, and you have to be able to set that up yourself or get some expert help.

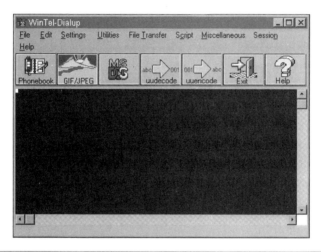

Figure 6.8 *WinTel lets you access a remote computer via Telnet.*

After you have logged on to an Archie server, you use the same commands described in the email section earlier, including the command **help** to find out what other commands are available. Using a program like WinTel to access and control an Archie server is an advanced topic beyond the scope of this book. I've included an example here because I want you to know what the possibilities are. If this is the only way that you can use Archie, I recommend that you find a good book on the subject.

SEARCH PHRASES

The success of your searches depends on the phrases you enter. You need to find out what features your search program offers. For example:

- Can you use wildcard characters such as * and ? in a search word? If so, what characters can you use and what do they mean?
- Can you use logical operators such as "and" and "or" between words? If so, what logical operators can you use and what do they mean?
- What happens if you use multiple words without logical operators?

You can usually find the answers to these questions by reading the documentation that accompanies your search software.

GOPHER

Gopher is another service where people can post information for you to read. Gopher is somewhat different from FTP and Usenet. Gopher is not set up for downloading files; it just displays them. Of course, after a file is displayed, your Gopher client probably will let you print it or save it on your hard disk. But it doesn't need to be decoded or scanned for viruses.

Gopher Menus

You find your way around Gopher via a series of menus, such as the one shown in Figure 6.9. The menu in the example lists several directories as well as several individual documents. If you click a directory, you see the next menu. If you click an

individual document, it appears on your screen. You will
sometimes find links to FTP and Web sites in Gopher menus.

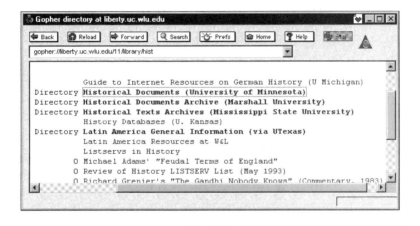

Figure 6.9 *Gopher is navigated through a series of menus.*

You can access Gopher from a Gopher client or from your
Web browser. If you want to use your Web browser, you turn
a Gopher address into a URL by inserting gopher:// in front of
it, as in gopher://liberty.uc.wlu.edu/11/library/hist.

Finding Gopher Sites with Veronica

FTP has its Archie, and Gopher has its Veronica. You use
Veronica to search Gopher menus for specific words. You
don't need any special software to access Veronica—you'll
find it listed in Gopher menus. For example, look at the first
item in the menu shown in Figure 6.10. Clicking that item
takes you to another directory where you can select items that
explain how to use Veronica and select various Veronica
search tools. Figure 6.11 shows the result of a search for the
phrase "Washington farewell." As you can see, several copies
of the farewell address were found in "gopherspace."

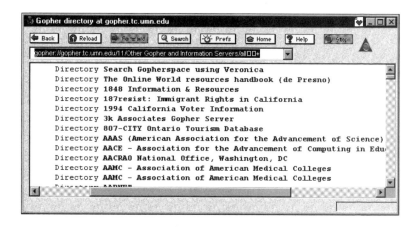

Figure 6.10 Many Gopher menus give you access to the Veronica search tool.

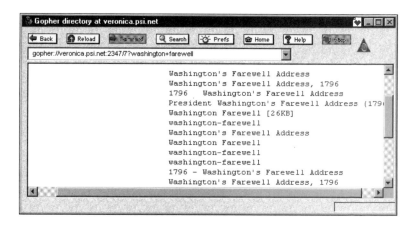

Figure 6.11 Veronica found many copies of Washington's farewell address.

You'll also see mention of two other Gopher search tools. Jughead is a variation of Veronica that lets you limit your search to a portion of Gopherspace. WAIS is an older search tool that is not used much anymore.

Usenet

Usenet provides a means whereby people can communicate with each other by posting messages and files on the electronic equivalent of a bulletin board, called a *newsgroup*. A *Usenet server* provides the software that maintains the bulletin board. You access the servers with a Usenet client program, known as a *newsreader*. Usenet is one of the Internet's most popular features, and your Internet access provider surely includes a built-in newsreader. But software libraries usually contain many downloadable newsreaders with advanced features.

Usenet is organized into categories such as alt (alternative), soc (society), and comp (computer). Within categories, there are topics such as alt.football, soc.adoption, and comp.databases. Each of those topics might have one or more newsgroups. A few topics have many newsgroups, but it's more common to find just a few newsgroups per topic.

The alt category tends to be home to the most off-the-wall newsgroups.

T I P

Most newsgroups are dedicated to a particular topic, such as quilting, the Society for Creative Anachronism, James Bond movies, Windows 95, or freedom of speech on the Internet. Anyone can post any message on a newsgroup, but people are supposed to stick to the topic. But if a newsgroup isn't moderated—meaning that someone or some group reads all the messages and eliminates the inappropriate ones—it soon fills up with off-topic messages such as "*****Get Rich Quick—No Kidding—It Really Works!!!!!!******" and "*** For a Great Time, Visit My Web Page***".

Off-topic messages, especially if they are *cross-posted* (posted to many boards), is known as *spam*. *Spammers* are people who *spam* the Internet with Usenet messages or email. When you spam a newsgroup, you're likely to get *flamed* (told off in no uncertain terms). And speaking of flaming, even moderated newsgroups often display courser language than most people are used to because many *Netizens* (citizens of the Internet) believe strongly in freedom of speech and will not censor a message simply because of its language or an antisocial or vulgar message.

READING NEWSGROUPS

Newsgroups go on for years and build up thousands of messages, even if someone removes old messages every so often. When you first access a newsgroup, you're faced with the daunting task of wading through all the messages you've never seen before. The message topics are supposed to help you select the messages that you want to read, but as you can see in Figure 6.12, many people don't do a very good job of assigning topics to their messages. So you end up having to read the message to find out what it's about. (Some people do that intentionally, of course.)

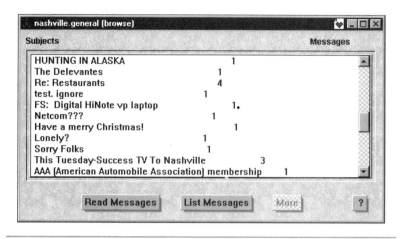

Figure 6.12 *Many message topics fail to communicate what the message is about.*

After you've caught up with old messages, you can tell your newsreader to just show you new messages. That way, you don't have to wade through all the ones you've already read. Of course, there's a way to get back to the old ones if you want. Figure 6.13 shows a typical example of a newsreader. In this example, if you click the **List Unread** button, you'll see a list of new messages, but the **List All** button shows you all the messages on the board, new and old. You can also mark all the messages as read, even though you didn't read them, by clicking **Mark Read**. That way, you can start off just reading new messages.

Read My Newsgroups

Internet Names   Mark All Newsgroups Read

My Newsgroups   Unread   Total

aol.motd	115	115
aol.newsgroups.bugs	355	355
aol.newsgroups.help	554	554
aol.newsgroups.suggestions	268	268
aol.newsgroups.test	853	853
comp.answers	569	569
news.announce.newusers	52	52
news.answers	2565	2565

List Unread   List All   Mark Read   Remove   More   ?

Figure 6.13 Most newsreaders give you a way to view all messages
or just the new ones.

T I P Reading and responding to messages online can consume hours of expensive Internet time. Most Internet service providers offer some means of signing on, grabbing new messages, downloading them to your hard drive, and then signing off again quickly. You read and respond to messages at your leisure and then sign on again just long enough to upload your responses. If your service doesn't include a built-in feature like this, you can probably find a program in your software library that will do it for you.

POSTING REPLIES

When you read a message, you might want to respond to it. Your newsreader probably provides a **Reply** button something like **Reply to Group** in the example in Figure 6.14. If you click that button, the message you post will be titled by default "Re: *topic*," as in "Re: How do I create a desktop shortcut?" Your message then becomes part of a *thread*—a series of messages following up one original message. Don't change the default topic, or people who are trying to follow the thread might miss your message.

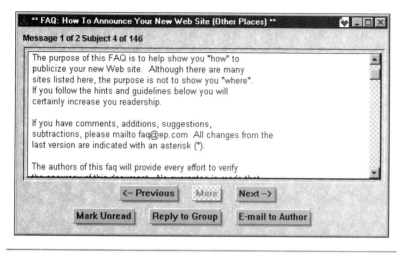

Figure 6.14 *When your newsreader displays a message, you have several choices of what to do next.*

When you reply to a message, you should quote the part of the message that you are responding to. That way, people who are just reading new messages don't have to search back to the previous message in the thread to find out what the heck you are talking about.

FOLLOWING THREADS

When you list the messages in a newsgroup, as in Figure 6.12, you only see the first message in each thread. The number next to the message tells you how many messages are in the thread. When you're reading a message, as in Figure 6.14, you can move forward and backward in the thread by clicking **Next** and **Previous**. When you reach the end or beginning of the thread, **Next** and **Previous** take you to the next thread. If you want to get out of the thread without reading all its messages, you would close the window and select another thread from the main newsgroup message list. (Your newsreader might work slightly differently and have different labels on its buttons, but its functions will be similar to these.)

DOWNLOADING FILES FROM NEWSGROUPS

As you learned in earlier chapters, you can't post binary information on Usenet. Nor can you post large messages. But you can encode binary files and split long files into several short ones. Hence, you can post software, graphics, sounds, and so on in newsgroups. Most newsgroups that permit such postings are in the alt.binaries category. Figure 6.15 shows a typical example— the messages at the bottom of the list are downloadable files.

Figure 6.15 *alt.binaries newsgroups often include downloadable files.*

When a message includes a downloadable file, your newsreader will provide some means to download it. In Figure

6.16, you would click the **Download File** or **Download Article** button. Many newsreaders will automatically decode the downloaded file for you.

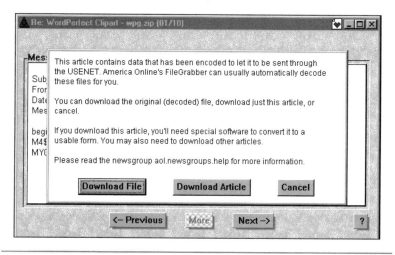

Figure 6.16 Your newsreader gives you some means to download files from a newsgroup.

Some newsreaders will even grab all the parts of a file automatically. With others, you have to make sure to download each part yourself. Most people who post a file in several parts label the parts with something like (1/5), (2/5), and so on, so that you can easily find them. You might have to scroll a bit to locate all the parts, as they are not always in sequence. Chapter 12 shows you how to assemble the parts into a single file again.

SOME HANDY INTERNET SITES

Winsite makes much software available for download. You'll find it at ftp.winsite.com or http://www.winsite.com.

You'll find a good entrance to Gopherspace at gopher://cwis.usc.edu/11/Other_Gophers_and_Information_ Resources/Gophers_by_Subject/Gopher_Jewels.

Another great Gopher menu is at gopher://gopher.tc.umn.edu/ 11/Other Gopher and Information Servers.

WHAT'S NEXT?

We've finished exploring the various ways of downloading files from the Internet. Now it's time to dig into the programs that we use to compress and decompress, encode and decode, split and reassemble, and scan for viruses. We'll start in the next chapter with one of the most popular archiving programs, WinZip.

PART III

Working with Compression and Encoding Programs

CHAPTER 7

Using WinZip

To me, the easiest way to zip and unzip files is with Niko Mak's WinZip. And as you saw in earlier chapters, it handles not only zip files, but also other archive and compression types such as TAR, Z, and GZ. I've included the shareware version of WinZip for Windows 95 on the disk that accompanies this book. This chapter gets you started using it.

What you'll learn in this chapter:

- More about WinZip's features
- How to install and uninstall WinZip
- How to zip files
- How to unzip files
- How to check unzipped files
- How to scan unzipped files for viruses
- How to try out new software via WinZip
- How to unzip a self-extracting archive
- How to add to WinZip's capabilities

NOTE   Windows 3.*x* users will have to suffer the term *folder* when working with WinZip. It means the same as *directory* and has replaced that word in Windows 95 and higher (it has been used in the Mac world for many years). WinZip uses it in its windows and help library, so I'll use it in this chapter too.

WHAT WINZIP CAN DO

I chose WinZip for this book for two reasons: it's full of great features, and I love its interface, which you can see in Figure 7.1. Both of these reasons are discussed in the following sections.

Name	Date	Time	Size	Ratio	Packed	Path
winzip.GID	11/11/96	07:00	33,462	84%	5,307	
order.txt	04/21/96	06:10	5,726	60%	2,263	
readme.txt	04/21/96	06:10	4,226	61%	1,642	
vendor.txt	04/21/96	06:10	4,101	57%	1,763	
license.txt	04/21/96	06:10	3,787	51%	1,853	
whatsnew.txt	04/21/96	06:10	2,977	56%	1,323	
sample.exe	02/29/96	00:00	656	35%	429	
file_id.diz	02/29/96	00:00	266	31%	183	

Selected 0 files, 0 bytes   Total 8 files, 54KB

Figure 7.1 WinZip's interface makes it easy to zip and unzip files.

WINZIP'S FEATURES

I'm just going to briefly introduce WinZip's features here because you'll be learning them in detail as this chapter progresses. But here's a quick summary:

- WinZip can unzip the following compression/archive formats on its own: PKZip, compress, gzip, and tar.

- It can unzip the following compression/archive formats with the help of extra software: ARC, ARJ, and LHArc.

- It can create zip files on its own, and it can create ARJ and LHArc archives with the help of extra software.

- With the assistance of PKZip, WinZip can create archives that span multiple disks, and it can create and unzip password-protected (encrypted) archives.

NOTE Microsoft has a compression format solely for the files on its distribution disks. Files compressed in Microsoft format usually have an underscore as the last character of the filename extension, as in **XCOPY.EX_**. Such files are meant to be installed only by DOS or Windows, so Microsoft doesn't publicize the details of its compression format, which changes frequently. Consequently, WinZip may or may not be able to unzip such files for you.

- You can create self-extracting WinZip archives with an additional program from Niko Mak.

- You can view many types of files before unzipping them.

- You can also run your virus scanner from within WinZip to check files before unzipping them.

- WinZip detects a Setup or Install file in an archive and lets you install and try out your newly unzipped software from within WinZip. It tracks the changes to your system made by the installation program so that, if you decide you don't like the new software, WinZip can uninstall it for you.

- WinZip keeps track of the folders where you usually store your archives, called your *Favorite Zip Folders*, and automatically lists the archives in those folders for you.

- WinZip can also help you find a lost archive—suppose that you downloaded a file without realizing where it was being stored on your hard drive—by searching for all the archives on your drives.

- In Windows 3.1, WinZip adds a menu to File Manager's menu bar that lets you apply WinZip functions, such as zip and unzip, to the files that you select in File Manager.

- In Windows 95 and higher, WinZip adds its functions to the context menu that pops up when you right-click files in My Computer and Explorer.

- You can also zip and unzip files by dragging and dropping them.

WinZip's Interface

WinZip actually has two interfaces: WinZip Classic, which you saw in Figure 7.1, and WinZip Wizard, shown in Figure 7.2. The wizard takes you step by step through the process of unzipping files. It's meant for beginners—experienced users tend to find it annoying. It's also limited; you can't zip files, and you can't unzip anything but zip files.

WinZip Classic lets you go through the steps on your own and is meant for more experienced users. It lets you zip and unzip in all the formats that WinZip handles, scan for viruses, try out new software, and completely control the entire procedure.

When you install WinZip, which is discussed next, you get to choose which interface you want to see each time you start it up. Most beginners should choose the wizard, and most experienced people should choose the Classic window. But don't agonize over this decision; it's easy to reverse it later on.

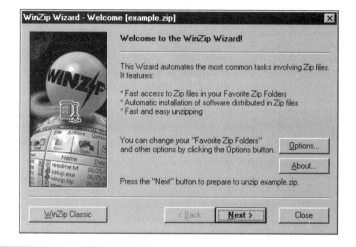

Figure 7.2 WinZip Wizard guides you through the process of unzipping files.

INSTALLING AND UNINSTALLING WINZIP

The disk for this book includes the Windows 95 version of Win Zip. If you need the Windows 3.1 version, you can download it from my Web site at http://members.aol.com/jnfbooks.

Follow these steps to install WinZip:

1. Remove the disk from the back of this book and insert it in drive A.

2. Choose **Start|Run** to open the Run dialog box.

3. Type **a:\winzip\setup** and press **Enter**. Setup asks for the name of the folder where WinZip should be installed, suggesting **C:\WinZip** as a default. You can change the name of the folder if you want, although most people don't.

4. When you're ready to proceed, click **OK**. Setup starts up a setup wizard and displays the first page, which is simply a list of WinZip's features.

5. Click **Next** to proceed. Setup asks you to agree to the license agreement. Read the license agreement before proceeding, if you haven't already done so. Here's how:

   a. Click **View License Agreement**. The license agreement appears.

   b. Scroll through and read the entire license agreement before continuing. Make sure that you know what you are agreeing to.

   c. When you are ready, click **Close** to close the license agreement.

6. Click **Yes** to agree to the license agreement. Setup asks for your registration information.

7. If you are installing from the disk included with this book, you are installing an unregistered version. Click **Continue Unregistered** to proceed. Next, you get to choose which interface you want to see each time you start WinZip.

8. Select either **WinZip Wizard** or **WinZip Classic** and click **Next**. Next, Setup will search your hard drive and determine your starting list of Favorite Zip Folders, which you can adapt later if you want. Right now, you must decide whether you want Setup to search the entire hard drive for your favorite zip folders or just to do a quick search.

9. Select either **Search Entire Hard Disk** or **Quick Search** and click **Next**. When it finishes its search, Setup displays the results.

10. Click **Next** to proceed. The Setup Wizard finishes its task by creating a WinZip program group (Windows 3.*x*) or by adding WinZip to your Start menu (Windows 95 and higher). On the final page of the wizard, you can choose whether you want to start up WinZip or quit for now.

11. Click either **Next** (to start up WinZip) or **Close** (to quit).

How to Uninstall WinZip

If you decide that you don't like WinZip and don't want to keep it on your system, don't just delete the WinZip folder. That would desert useless bits and pieces of WinZip throughout your system. The WinZip menu would remain on File Manager's file bar, for example. Instead, you should *uninstall* WinZip. You uninstall the 16-bit version of WinZip by opening the WinZip program group and double-clicking the **Uninstall WinZip** icon. For the 32-bit version, choose **Start|Programs|WinZip|Uninstall WinZip**. In both cases, you'll be asked to confirm your decision (in case you got there accidentally).

Unzipping Files

Because the wizard is a snap, I'll show you that first. Then you'll learn all the extra options you get with the classic interface.

Unzipping Files with WinZip Wizard

If the wizard is the default interface, you'll see it as soon as you start up WinZip. But if WinZip Classic is your default, you must click the **Wizard** button at the right end of the button bar (you can see it in Figure 7.1) to get to the wizard.

When you start WinZip Wizard, you see an introductory page (refer back to Figure 7.2). When you click **Next,** WinZip does a search and lists all the zip files in your Favorite Zip Folders. Figure 7.3 shows an example.

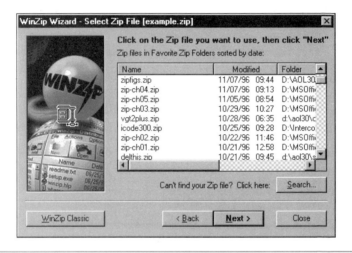

Figure 7.3 WinZip Wizard lists all the zip files in your Favorite Zip Folders.

Notice the message immediately above the list: "Zip files in Favorite Zip Folders sorted by date." This tells you that the archives are listed from the newest to the oldest, on the assumption that you probably want to unzip your newest archive. You can change the order very simply—just click the header above the desired column. For example, to sort by name, click the word **Name** above the first column. The first time you click it, the files are sorted in ascending order by name. Click it again to reverse the order. The same is true for the **Modified** and **Folder** columns. The message above the list changes to indicate how the files are currently sorted.

If the file you want isn't in the list, click the **Search** button to open the dialog box shown in Figure 7.4. As you can see, you can search all your drives, select a drive to search, search your Favorite Zip Folders (which the wizard already did), or look for the archive on your own in a common Windows browse dialog box. The search results are displayed in the wizard's window, as shown in Figure 7.3.

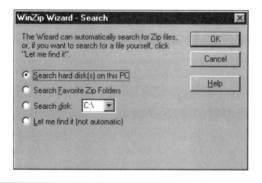

Figure 7.4 You use this dialog box to search for an archive to unzip.

When you have found the archive you want to unzip, select it and click **Next**. On the next page of the wizard, shown in Figure 7.5, you get to choose the folder to receive the unzipped files. The default is a folder that WinZip creates, called **c:\unzipped***filename*. For example, if you are unzipping a file called **mynovel.zip**, the default folder is **c:\unzipped\mynovel**.

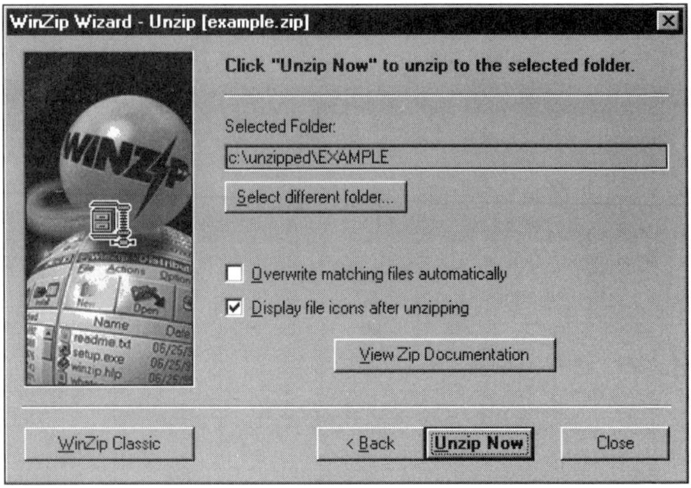

Figure 7.5 On this page, you identify the folder to receive the unzipped files.

Suppose that you don't like the default folder and you click the **Select Different Folder** button. Figure 7.6 shows the dialog box that appears. Here, you can browse through your drives and select an existing folder or click the **New** button to create a new folder. When you have established the folder to receive the unzipped files, you click the **OK** button to return to the wizard; then click the **Unzip Now** button to unzip the archive.

After it finishes unzipping, WinZip opens a window showing the unzipped files so that you can access them easily. The last page of the wizard lets you exit WinZip (by clicking **Close**) or start over again with another archive (by clicking **Next**).

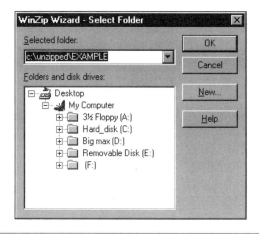

Figure 7.6 *You can browse for an existing folder or create a new one in this dialog box.*

If the target folder already contains files with the same names as the ones being unzipped, WinZip asks if you want to replace the existing files with the unzipped ones.

NOTE

Starting up WinZip on its own and then selecting an archive is not the only way to unzip an archive. You can start by selecting the archive with one of these techniques:

- In a directory window such as Windows 3.*x* File Manager or Windows 95 My Computer, open a ZIP archive. WinZip's Setup associated the **.zip** extension with WinZip, so opening the archive automatically starts up WinZip.

How to open an archive (these are standard Windows techniques for opening any kind of file):

- Double-click it.

- Select it and press **Enter**.

- Right-click it and choose **Open** from the context menu (Windows 95 and higher)

- Drag an archive from a directory window to the open WinZip window.

- In a directory window, drag an archive and drop it on the WinZip program icon.

- In Windows 3.*x* File Manager, select an archive and then choose **Open Archive** from the WinZip menu, shown in Figure 7.7.

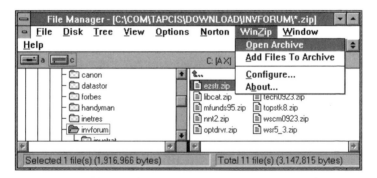

Figure 7.7 *WinZip adds this menu to File Manager's menu bar.*

All these methods open the archive along with WinZip, so you don't have to select the archive on page 2 of the wizard. The wizard skips from page 1 to page 3, where you choose the folder to receive the unzipped files.

One more way of starting WinZip in Windows 95 or higher doesn't even involve the wizard because there are no more decisions to be made—you can use your right mouse button to drag an archive from one folder to another. When you drop the archive, a context menu pops up containing an **Extract To** option. When you choose **Extract To,** WinZip starts up and extracts the archive to the folder where you dropped it.

That's all there is to unzipping archives with WinZip Wizard. As you'll see in the next section, it's almost as easy to unzip with WinZip Classic, but you do have many more options if you want them.

Unzipping with WinZip Classic

When you start WinZip Classic without an archive, its client area is blank, and most of its buttons are disabled, as shown in Figure 7.8. You click the **Open** button to browse for an archive that you want to unzip. The Classic interface does not use the Favorite Zip Folders feature—that's for the Wizard only—so you can't ask WinZip to search for a lost archive unless you switch to the wizard.

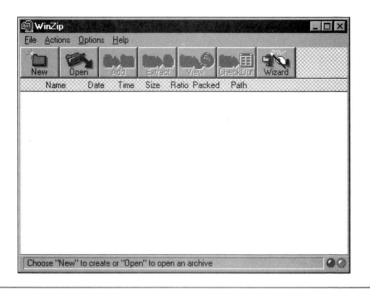

Figure 7.8 *When no archive is selected, WinZip Classic looks like this.*

The wizard has a **WinZip Classic** button, and WinZip Classic has a **Wizard** button so that you can toggle easily between the two interfaces.

T I P

After you open an archive, its contents are displayed in the Classic window, as shown in Figure 7.9. As with the wizard, you can change the sort order of the list by clicking a column head. But unlike the wizard, you can't reverse the order by clicking the same column head again. The Name column always sorts the list in ascending order; the other columns always sort the list in descending order.

Clicking either **Date** or **Time** sorts the list by the date. Items with the same date are sorted by time.

T I P

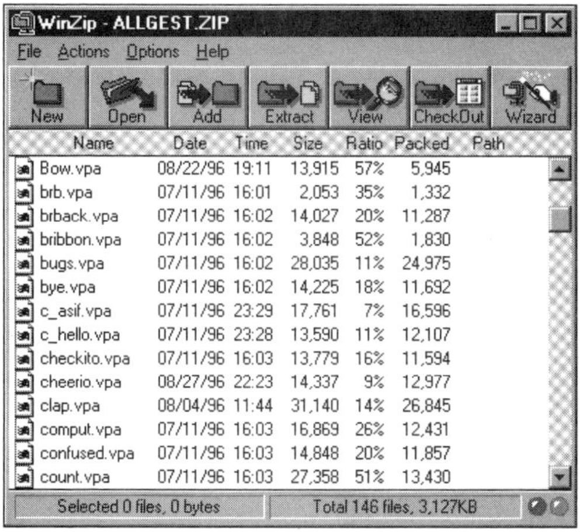

Figure 7.9 *WinZip lists the contents of the open archive in the Classic window.*

If you want to unzip the entire archive, just click the **Extract** button. But you don't have to unzip all the files in the archive. If you select one or more files before clicking **Extract**, you have the option of unzipping just those files. In either case, the dialog box shown in Figure 7.10 appears. (Figure 7.10 shows the Windows 95 version. The Windows 3.*x* version is similar.)

Figure 7.10 *This dialog box appears when you click the **Extract** button.*

A quick way to extract one or more files is to drag them out of the WinZip window. You could drop files into your Microsoft Word window, for example, or into another folder in your Explorer window.

T I P

Notice the group of option buttons labeled **Files**. Here, you can choose whether you want to unzip all the files, just the selected files, or the file(s) that match a particular filename, such as **chap05*.***. Use standard DOS wildcards (* and ?) to create the filename.

The **Selected Files** option is not available if no files are selected.

N O T E

You also can indicate in this dialog box where the unzipped files should go. The **Extract To** box identifies the target folder. By default, it shows the last folder that you unzipped files to. Its drop-down list displays all the folders that you have used recently; you can select one of those if you want. If you don't want any of those folders, you can type the pathname of the desired folder in the box, or you can use the **Folders/Drives** box to select the target folder.

It's easy to ignore the **Extract To** box; but if you do, you won't know where WinZip put your unzipped files. Always pay attention to where the files are going, especially when you accept the default location.

T I P

People often want to create a new folder to receive a set of unzipped files. You can do that by clicking the **New Folder** button, which pops up a dialog box where you can type a name for the new folder. That folder then appears in the **Extract To** box.

When the target folder already contains files, there could be a problem with an unzipped file replacing an existing file of the same name. This may or may not be desirable, depending on what the files are. Normally, WinZip asks you before replacing a file; you have to approve or deny the replacement. But if you know that you want to replace the existing files with the new ones, you can check the **Overwrite Existing Files** option so that you don't have to confirm each replacement individually.

When someone zips up files from more than one folder, the names of the source folders are included in the ZIP file. If you want WinZip to create those same folders on your system, be sure to check **Use Folder Names**. Otherwise, all the files will be unzipped into the folder you identify in the **Extract To** box, regardless of where they come from. **Use Folder Names** is selected by default because that's the correct choice most of the time.

Any new folder names that WinZip creates become subfolders under the target folder.

NOTE

When you've made all the choices you want, click the **Extract** button to extract the files. You'll see a progress bar at the bottom right of the Classic window as the files are unzipped. If you change your mind after starting the job, you can interrupt it by clicking anywhere in the window. A small dialog box pops up asking whether you want to continue or abort the job.

When the job is done, the current archive remains open on your screen. You can choose more files to extract, open a different archive, or choose some of WinZip's other functions. Of course, you can also exit WinZip if you're finished with it for the time being.

VIEWING FILES

Suppose that you have downloaded an archive and you're not sure which files you want to extract, if any. You can view the files before you unzip them. This comes in especially handy in viewing Readme files before extracting and installing software. To view a file, select it and choose **Actions|View** (shortcut key **Ctrl+V**). The dialog box shown in Figure 7.11 lets you indicate what software should be used to display the file:

- **Associated Program** refers to whatever program is associated with the file's type (as indicated by its extension) on your system. In the example in Figure 7.11, it's Windows Paint.

- **Internal ASCII Text Viewer** uses WinZip's own viewer to display ASCII text, which makes sense only if the file actually contains ASCII text. Otherwise, you'll see something like Ós+[_q2fíÃJ®.

- **Viewer** lets you select your own viewer if you don't like the associated one. For example, if the file is a **.doc** file and you want to view it with Microsoft Word but it's associated with Windows Write, you would choose the third option and select Microsoft Word as the viewer. You can type the pathname of the appropriate program file, select it from the drop-down list if it's there, or click the button next to **Viewer** to open a browse dialog box so that you can locate and select it.

Figure 7.11 *This dialog box appears when you choose the*
ActionsⅠView command.

Another way to view a file is to double-click it in the Classic window, which automatically calls up the associated program as the viewer.

Double-clicking an executable file causes it to be unzipped and executed.

WARNING

A file actually can't be displayed before it is unzipped. When you use WinZip's view feature, WinZip has to unzip the file temporarily so that it can be displayed. It erases the temporary version when you close the viewer. But if you modify the file while viewing it, WinZip lets you save the changes back into the zipped version if you want.

CHECKING FOR VIRUSES

Before you unzip and use new files, you might want to check them for viruses. You can ask WinZip to do this for you, using whatever virus scanner you have installed on your system. Just choose **Actions|Virus Scan** or press **Ctrl+S**. WinZip unzips the files to a temporary folder, scans them, shows you the results of the scan (using the virus scanner's report), and then deletes unzipped files from the temporary folder.

It doesn't matter whether you have already unzipped the archive—WinZip will still unzip it into a temporary folder to scan it.

NOTE

How does WinZip know what virus scanner you have? It will actually search your system for the most popular scanners:

> Central Point Desktop for Windows (WNAVPIR and CPAV)
> Dr. Solomon's Anti-Virus Toolkit
> Frisk (F-PROT)
> McAfee (SCAN and WSCAN)
> Microsoft Antivirus (MSAV)
> Norton Antivirus (NAV and NAVW)
> ThunderByte (TBSCAN)

WinZip can use all those scanners automatically. If your scanner isn't on the list, you will have to configure WinZip to work with your scanner. For detailed instructions on how to do that, look up "Virus Scanner Configuration" in WinZip's help library.

NOTE WinZip searches for virus scanners only in those folders listed in your system's PATH command. If you have one of the scanners listed above but WinZip can't find it, its folder must not be in your system path. You can fix the problem by choosing **Options|Program Locations** and choosing your scanner in the drop-down list for Virus Scanner. Then add the correct path to the name of the scanner.

TRYING OUT NEW SOFTWARE

If you're like me, you download a lot of software—especially games—just to try it out. If you decide not to keep it, you could have trouble removing all of it from your system again. It might have installed DLLs in your Windows folders, added settings to your INI files and system registry, and so on. These tidbits are not always easy to identify and get rid of.

But WinZip includes a feature that lets you try out new software and remove it easily. WinZip keeps track of all the changes made by the Install or Setup program. If you want to uninstall it, WinZip reverses *all* of them for you. Here's how it works. When you open an archive that contains a **Setup.exe** or **Install.exe** file, WinZip assumes that the archive contains installable software. It enables the **Install** option on your **Actions** menu. In Windows 3.*x*, it also adds an **Install** button to the button bar.

When you choose the **Install** option, the dialog box shown in Figure 7.12 appears. As you can see in the dialog box, WinZip will unzip the archive to a temporary folder and then run the Setup or Install program. If you select **Save Configuration Info for Possible Uninstall**, WinZip keeps track of what is installed.

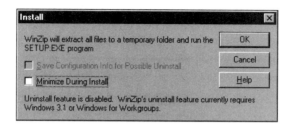

Figure 7.12 This dialog box appears when you click Install.

WinZip stays open while the new software is running. Select **Minimize During Install** to minimize WinZip's window. The minimized icon will stay on top so that you can find WinZip easily when you're ready to indicate whether you want to keep or uninstall the new software.

After the installation, run the new program. Try it out to your heart's content. When you exit the program, go back to WinZip and indicate whether you want to keep or uninstall the software. If you decide to uninstall it, WinZip lets you choose exactly what changes you want to remove.

WARNING

WinZip's uninstall feature keeps track of *all* changes to your system from the moment it started the Install or Setup program. If you interrupted the tryout to make a few notes on your word processor, check and answer your email, and update a spreadsheet, those changes would also be removed from the system. So when you're using WinZip's tryout feature, stick to the tryout and don't do anything else.

INVALID COMPRESSION TYPES

Of the millions of people who use the Internet, a few don't know what they're doing. They notice that other people's filenames end in **.zip**, so they end their filenames with **.zip** too.

Consequently, not every file ending in **.zip** is a valid zip file; nor is every **.z** file a valid gzip file; nor every **.lzh** file a valid LHArc file. If you try to open an archive in WinZip and get the message "Cannot open file; it does not appear to be a valid archive," you have probably run into one of these strange ducks. Chapter 11 explores some things you can do to find out what the file really is.

ZIPPING FILES

Suppose that you are ready to send a chapter to your editor and you want to zip all the files involved into one zip file. You begin by starting WinZip. Then you click the **New** button to open the dialog box shown in Figure 7.13. (Figure 7.13 shows the Windows 95 version of the New Archive dialog box.) You give the archive a name and identify a folder for it.

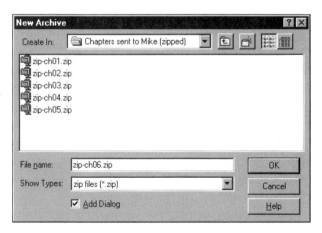

Figure 7.13 *You assign a name and a location for your new archive in this dialog box.*

T I P   The new archive's extension determines the type of compression. If you leave it blank or name it **.zip**, PKZip format is used. You can also name it **.arj** for ARJ format or **.lhz** for LHArc format, but only if you have installed the necessary support software. If you name it **.gz**, **.z**, **.arc**, and so on, you'll get an error message because WinZip can't do those types of compression.

If you leave the **Add Dialog** option checked, when you click **OK**, the dialog box shown in Figure 7.14 appears. In this dialog box, you select the files to be zipped into the new archive. You can select multiple files but only from one folder. When you click the **Add** button, the files are zipped into the new archive and you return to the Classic window, where you can see the list of files in the archive. If you now want to add more files from other folders, click the **Add** button to return to the Add dialog box.

Figure 7.14 You select the files to be zipped from this dialog box.

You can add files to any open archive using the **Add** button, even an archive that you received from someone else, one that was not created by WinZip, or one that you created several years ago.

TIP

As you can see in Figure 7.14, you have several options in the Add dialog box:

- You can type a generic filename using DOS wildcards in the **File Name** box and then click **Add With Wildcards** to add all files from the current folder that match the generic filename. (If you just click **Add**, WinZip simply filters the list of files in the list box to show only ones that match the generic filename.)
- The **Action** drop-down list provides several action alternatives when you click the **Add** or **Add With Wildcards** button:
  - **Add** adds the selected files to the archive (the default).
  - **Freshen** replaces files already in the archive with new copies of the selected files.
  - **Move** adds the selected files to the archive and then deletes them from their original folder.
  - **Update** is the same as freshen, except any selected files that aren't already in the archive are added.
- You can choose from several levels of **Compression:**
  - **Normal:** A compromise between speed and space
  - **Maximum:** Takes extra time to compress the files to be as small as possible; the slowest method
  - **Fast:** Faster than Normal compression, but results in larger files

- **Superfast:** Even faster and larger than Fast
- **None:** No compression (really, really fast)
- With the **Recurse Folders** option, WinZip looks in all subfolders of the current folder for files that match the specified filename, even if it is a single filename, not a generic one. For example, suppose that you want to zip all the files in the current folder plus all its subfolders. You would specify a generic filename of *.* and check the **Recurse Folders** option.
- **Save Extra Folder Info** stores any folder pathname specified in **File Name**. This can be an important option if you are adding files from several different folders in separate Add actions, and you want those folder names to carry through to the recipient's drive—as when you are zipping software for distribution.
- Use **Store Filenames in DOS 8.3 Form** if you're using Windows 95 or higher and have taken advantage of the long filename feature, but you only want the short DOS filenames to be stored in the archive.
- **Multiple Disk Spanning** lets you create an archive that is so large that it requires more than one floppy disk. This option is available only if you have installed PKZip 2.04 and have told WinZip where to find it via the **Options|Program Locations** command.

OTHER WAYS TO ZIP FILES

There are a number of other ways to zip one or more files without selecting them from the Add dialog box. You can, for example, select some files in File Manager and then choose **Zip** from the WinZip menu. Or in Windows 95, you can right-click some files in Explorer and then choose **Add to Zip** from the context menu. WinZip starts up (unless it was already running) and displays a dialog box that lets you choose the archive and Add options such as **Compression** and **Recurse Folders**. Dragging a file and dropping it on the WinZip window or the WinZip program icon has the same result.

Perhaps the easiest way to add files to an existing archive is simply to drag and drop them on the archive in a directory window such as File Manager or Explorer. This runs WinZip just long enough to compress the files; no dialogs boxes or windows open. If you have a really fast system, you might find yourself opening the archive just to make sure that the files were really added.

Removing Files from an Archive

If you decide to remove some files from an archive, all you have to do is select them in the archive list and press the **Delete** key. WinZip asks you to confirm the deletion. This deletes the files from the archive only, not from their original folder.

Some Things You Might Want to Explore on Your Own

After you're comfortable with the basics of WinZip, you might want to explore some of its more advanced options:

- The Check Out feature gives you a facility that's kind of halfway between unzipping and trying out. It unzips the files to a program group, which makes it easy to view the documents and try out the programs. (In Windows 95 and higher, the program group becomes a Start menu item.) When you're finished, you can keep or remove the program group. See "Check Out" in the WinZip help library for more information.

- You can create self-extracting WinZip files if you add an extra program called the WinZip Self-Extractor. See "WinZip Self-Extractor" in the WinZip help library for more information.

- You can create self-extracting DOS files, just like PKZip self-extracting files, by choosing **Actions|Make .EXE File**. See "Self-Extracting Zip Files" in the WinZip help library for more information.

- WinZip has a number of options that you can set to change the way it works. For example, you can ask it to beep after a long zipping operation so that you don't have to sit there and watch it to know when it's done. Explore the Options menu to find out what options are available to you. (All the options are explained in the help library.)

WHAT'S NEXT?

Now that you know how to use WinZip, we'll turn our attention to the original PKZip in the next chapter. It is also included on the disk that accompanies this book.

CHAPTER 8

Using PKZip

Now that you've learned how to use WinZip for your basic archiving and extracting tasks, it's time to see what PKZip itself has to offer. You'll find that it can do many things that WinZip can't, although its DOS interface is a lot less comfortable.

NOTE PKZip's manual deals with the question, "Why is this program so complicated?" Their answer (in part): "The people using PKZIP were mostly hobbyists with a fair amount of computer experience. PKZip was designed to be powerful and fast. Someone who is familiar with the workings of PKZIP can be very efficient with the command line."

Actually, PKZip is one of a related set of programs, which I call the PKZip *family*. The entire family is the subject of this chapter.

What you'll learn in this chapter:

- What the PKZip family can do
- How to install the software
- How to create and update archives
- How to find out what's in an archive
- How to extract all or part of an archive (including self-extracting archives)
- How to create a self-extracting archive

- How to choose a compression level
- How to add comments to an archive
- How to encrypt and decrypt files in an archive
- How to test the integrity of the files in an archive
- How to repair a corrupted archive
- How to use the manual that accompanies the software

In the WinZip chapter, Windows 3.*x* users had to deal with the term *folder* rather than *directory*. Now the tables are turned. PKZip and its siblings, being DOS programs, use the term *directory*, so I will follow suit in this chapter.

NOTE

WHAT THE PKZIP FAMILY CAN DO

The PKZip family includes PKZip itself for zipping archives, PKUnzip and PKUnzip Junior for unzipping, ZIP2EXE for creating self-extracting archives, and PKZipFix for fixing corrupted archives.

Two minor programs also are included only in the registered version: PKConfig for changing PKZip's default configuration and PKSafeANSI for preventing ANSI "bombs." (An ANSI "bomb" redefines your keyboard so that you can't type normally. It's a pain in the neck perpetrated by the same folks who bring you viruses and trojan horses.) Because these two programs are not included in the shareware version that accompanies this book, I won't cover them here.

NOTE

PKZip can do all the things you'd expect it to: create a new archive, add files to it, delete files from it, and list its contents. You'll also find a wide variety of options:

N O T E   In the following list, items marked with * are covered in this chapter. Items marked with # are not covered, either because they are advanced options or because they are not especially useful in handling files over the Internet. All the options are documented in the manual included with the PKZip software.

* You can select from a variety of compression methods, from Zero to Maximum.

* You can ask PKZip to update an archive with any files that you have created or modified since the last time you updated the archive.

* You can add comments for the archive itself and for each of the files it includes.

* PKZip will encrypt private files so that no one can decrypt them without the correct password.

\# It will create an archive that spans multiple floppy disks.

\# It can record the pathnames of the source directories so that they can be re-created when the archive is unzipped.

\# It will recurse subdirectories.

\# Several options are designed to let PKZip act as your main backup tool. You can, for example, tell PKZip to add only those files with a positive archive attribute.

\# You have quite a bit of control over the attributes of the archived files. You can, for example, retain or clear the hidden, system, and read-only attributes in the archive.

\# Rather than type out the list of filenames every time you update an archive, you can keep the list in a separate file, called a *list file*, and tell PKZip to use the list file.

\# PKZip can include Authenticity Verification information so that the recipient can tell if an archive has been tampered with after it was zipped. (Authenticity Verification requires obtaining an AV serial number from PKWare.)

What PKZip can't do, of course, is unzip archives. You need PKUnzip or PKUnzip Junior for that. PKUnzip also has many options, although not nearly as many as PKZip:

*   PKUnzip includes the same information viewing feature as PKZip, so you can find out about the files in an archive before you unzip them.

*   You can unzip the entire archive or select specific files to unzip.

*   You can ask PKUnzip to update your hard drive with any files from the archive that are newer.

*   PKUnzip will ask for permission to overwrite existing files as it unzips, or you can tell it to always overwrite or never overwrite existing files.

*   You can test the integrity of the archived files.

*   You can specify a password to unzip encrypted files.

\#   PKUnzip can re-create the original directory structure when unzipping (if pathname information is included in the archive).

\#   You can use a list file to specify which files to unzip.

\#   PKUnzip can maintain or ignore the attributes of archived files.

\#   You can extract files to devices other than your disk drives: printer, monitor, or serial port.

The junior version of PKUnzip loads faster and uses less memory, so naturally it offers fewer options. It always extracts the entire archive—you can't select files to be unzipped—and only the overwrite option is available.

You use ZIP2EXE to convert a zip archive into a self-extracting archive and vice versa. Its only option is whether you want a full-featured archive or a junior archive. If you create a full-featured archive, then the recipient can use many of the PKUnzip options when unzipping it. A junior archive is limited to the same unzipping options as PKUnzip Junior.

PKZipFix is a special program that might help if you encounter a corrupted zip archive. Usually, PKUnzip will identify a corrupted file and suggest that you use PKZipFix.

Also included on your shareware disk is a manual, stored as a DOS text document called **manual.doc**. Some sections of the complete manual are omitted from the shareware version, but all the essential sections on the programs and their options are intact.

THE CURRENT PKZIP VERSION

This book includes the latest shareware release of the PKZip family, release 2.04g. If you have an earlier version, you would be wise to upgrade to 2.04g because earlier versions are not compatible with the improved compression method, called *deflating*, used by release 2.04. Earlier releases of PKZip can't extract files from an archive created by release 2.04.

WARNING

If you see an even newer release of PKZip, in particular version 3.0 or higher, be very wary. Several trojan horses are floating around on the Internet pretending to be new releases of PKZip. I don't know of any plans for a legitimate release beyond PKZip 2.04 for the near future.

Installing the PKZip Family

I'm going to assume—and I hope I'm correct—that you prefer to work in Windows, as I do. I'll show you how to install and run PKZip using Windows' DOS prompt.

PKZip and its siblings arrive in a self-extracting file. The first step in installing them is to unzip them. The following procedure extracts them into a directory called **C:\PKWare**. Feel free to adapt the procedure to use a different drive and directory if you want.

 You'll need approximately half a megabyte of disk space (about 560K) to extract the shareware version of PKZip.

NOTE

How to install PKZip and its siblings:

1. Insert the disk from the back of this book into drive A.
2. In Windows 3.*x* Program Manager, open the Main group and then double-click **MS-DOS Prompt** to open the DOS window.

    or

    In Windows 95 and higher, choose **Start|Programs|MS-DOS Prompt** to open the DOS window.
3. Enter the following command to change to drive C if necessary:

        c:

4. Enter the following command to create the C:\PKWare directory:

```
md c:\PKWare
```

Windows 95 pays attention to the capitalization of a new directory, so I intentionally used caps in the preceding command. In Windows 3.x, the name will appear as PKWARE regardless of how you type it in the MD command.

T I P

5. Enter the following command to change to the new directory:

    ```
    cd c:\pkware
    ```

6. Enter the following command to unzip the PK archive into the current directory:

    ```
    a:\pkz204g
    ```

    You should see the list of files being unzipped, as shown below.

```
MS-DOS Prompt                                          _ □ ✕

Searching EXE: C:/PKWARE/PKZ204G.EXE
  Inflating: README.DOC      -AV
  Inflating: SHAREWAR.DOC    -AV
  Inflating: WHATSNEW.204    -AV
  Inflating: V204G.NEW       -AV
  Inflating: HINTS.TXT       -AV
  Inflating: LICENSE.DOC     -AV
  Inflating: ORDER.DOC       -AV
  Inflating: ADDENDUM.DOC    -AV
  Inflating: MANUAL.DOC      -AV
  Inflating: AUTHVERI.FRM    -AV
  Inflating: PKZIP.EXE       -AV
  Inflating: PKUNZIP.EXE     -AV
  Inflating: PKZIPFIX.EXE    -AV
  Inflating: ZIP2EXE.EXE     -AV
  Inflating: PKUNZJR.COM     -AV
  Inflating: OMBUDSMN.ASP    -AV

Authentic files Verified!   # PKW655
PKWARE Inc.

Thank you for using PKWARE!  PKWARE Support BBS (414) 354-8670

C:\PKWare>
```

PKZip works better if you add its directory to your DOS search path. Here's how:

1. In the DOS window, enter the following command to open your **AUTOEXEC.BAT** file for editing:

    ```
    edit autoexec.bat
    ```

2. Find the line containing the PATH command. It will look something like the following line, although your pathnames might be different:

    ```
    PATH C:\WINDOWS;C:WINDOWS\COMMAND;C:\WINDOWS\SYSTEM
    ```

WARNING

Do not edit your PATH command to look like the preceding example. In fact, do not change anything in your **autoexec.bat** file except as described in the following steps.

3. Add a semicolon (;) to the end of the PATH command unless there already is one.

4. Add the following to the end of the line, after the semicolon:

    ```
    c:\pkware
    ```

5. Choose **File|Save**.

6. Choose **File|Exit**.

7. Enter the following command to close the DOS window:

    ```
    Exit
    ```

8. Close all other windows.

9. In Windows 3.*x*, exit Windows, reboot, and restart or in Windows 95 and higher, choose **Start|Shut Down**, select **Restart the Computer**, and click **Yes**.

Your PKZip software is now ready to go. If you want to remove it from your hard drive again, just erase the PKWare directory and delete the tail that you added to your PATH command.

ENTERING DOS COMMANDS

You must enter DOS commands to use PKZip. But you don't have to leave Windows—there are several ways to enter DOS commands under Windows. I like using the DOS window best of all because then I can run several PKZip and PKUnzip commands in succession, which I often find necessary. So throughout this chapter, I'm assuming that you already have a DOS window open. Just in case you're not sure how to do that, here's a reminder:

- In Windows 3.*x* Program Manager, open **Main** and then open **MS-DOS Prompt**.
- In Windows 95 and higher, choose **Start|Programs|MS-DOS Prompt**.

PKZIP FAMILY COMMANDS

The PKZip family use commands with this general structure:

```
program [options] archive [files]
```

Square brackets [ ] indicate that an item is optional. The name of the *program* and the name of the *archive* are required, but *options* and *files* are not required. You'll see why as the chapter progresses.

T I P

Program identifies the program you want to use, such as PKZip or PKUnzip. For example, if you want to create an archive called **family.zip**, you could enter this command, where pkzip is the name of the program:

```
pkzip family.zip
```

Options are expressions that identify the options you want to use. An option usually begins with a hyphen followed by a single character, such as *-v* to view information or *-&* to span floppy disks. Some options have several settings, and you choose a particular setting by adding another character, as in *-vb* to view brief information, *-vc* to view comments, or *-vt* to view technical information. Some options require text after the single character, as in *-selmerfudd* to apply the password *elmerfudd* to an archive.

T I P   If you're used to DOS commands, you're used to using a slash (/) instead of a hyphen on command options. You can use slashes with the PKZip family too, but because all the PKWare documentation uses hyphens, I'll use hyphens in this chapter.

Archive is the pathname of the archive. If it's in the current directory, you can omit the path and just use the filename alone. If it's in another directory, you need to include the path. The following command unzips an archive named **newfiles.zip** located in the **c:\download** directory.

```
pkunzip c:\download\newfiles
```

T I P   With PKWare, the extension **.zip** is the default, so you can always omit **.zip** from an archive name. You can assign other extensions to your archive names, but I think that's a bad practice, so you won't see any examples in this book.

Files represents the pathnames of the files to be archived or unzipped. You can use a specific pathname, as in the following command, which adds a file named **update.txt** to the archive named **report4.zip**:

```
pkzip report4.zip update.txt
```

For multiple files, you can use a generic pathname. The following example extracts all the files matching the generic name **.doc* from the archive named **backup.zip** to the current directory:

```
pkunzip backup *.doc
```

You can also use a series of single or generic pathnames, separated by commas. In the following example, several files from the current directory are added to the archive named **oldreps.zip**:

```
pkzip oldreps *.rep, correct.txt, altern.txt, rep*.doc,
old*.doc, old*.txt
```

The DOS command line is limited to 127 characters, or about 1.5 lines on an 80-column monitor. If you need more filenames than that, you'll have to use additional commands.

T I P

THE BASICS

The basic functions of PKZip and PKUnzip pretty much duplicate what you have already learned to do with WinZip. But there are differences, so it's worth spending some time reviewing the basics.

CREATING ARCHIVES

Suppose that you want to zip all the files in the current directory into an archive named **alltexts.zip**. When you don't specify any files, PKZip assumes that you want them all, so either of the following commands would work:

```
pkzip alltexts *.*
```

```
pkzip alltexts
```

Figure 8.1 shows the information that PKZip displays when it creates a new archive. The first set of lines displays version and copyright information. The next set of lines tells you what key features PKZip found in your system. (Yours might be different from mine. PKZip seems to think my computer is a 486. It's a Pentium. Honest.) Next PKZip tells you whether it created a new archive or updated an existing one. In this example, it created a new one because it couldn't find an existing **alltexts.zip** in the current directory. The remaining lines list the files that were zipped into the archive, along with their compression ratios. The word *deflating* represents PKZip's compression method.

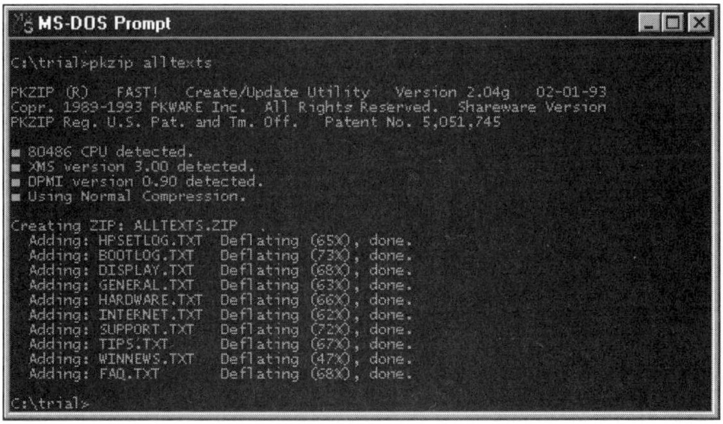

Figure 8.1 *PKZip's report shows which files were added to the archive.*

ADDING TO ARCHIVES

Now suppose that you want to add three more files to **alltexts.zip** with this command:

```
pkzip alltexts doc1.txt doc2.txt tips.txt
```

Figure 8.2 shows what happens when you enter the command. As you can see, rather than saying "Creating," it says "Updating" because **alltexts.zip** already exists. The line for **tips.txt** also says "Updating" rather than "Adding." That's because **alltexts.zip** already contained a file named **tips.txt,** which was replaced by the new one.

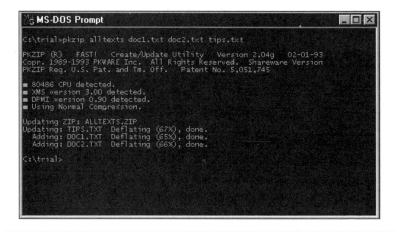

Figure 8.2 This report shows files being added to an existing archive.

ADDING FILES FROM OTHER DIRECTORIES

Your source files don't have to be in the current directory. You can add files from other directories by including paths with their filenames, as in:

```
pkzip alltexts \texts\*.txt \docs\*.txt \olddocs\*.txt
```

DELETING FILES FROM ARCHIVES

Now suppose that you want to remove one or more files from the archive. You need to use the -d option, which deletes specified files. Figure 8.3 shows what happens when you enter this command:

```
pkzip -d alltexts doc*.txt tips.txt style.txt
```

The report shows you exactly which files were deleted, in this case **doc1.txt, doc2.txt,** and **tips.txt.** Notice that **style.txt** is not in the list of deleted files, so apparently it was not in the archive. PKZip doesn't warn you about individual files that weren't added or deleted. It only warns you when *no* files were added or deleted, when it crows "nothing to do!" So you might want to develop the habit of actually reading that file list to make sure that you didn't somehow miss a file.

Figure 8.3 *When you use the -d option, PKZip deletes files from the archive.*

FINDING OUT WHAT'S IN AN ARCHIVE

By the time you've added and deleted a few files, you might be confused about what's in an archive. You can list its contents with the -v option, as shown in Figure 8.4. Another time to use -v is when you receive an archive from someone else and want to know what's in it before you unzip it.

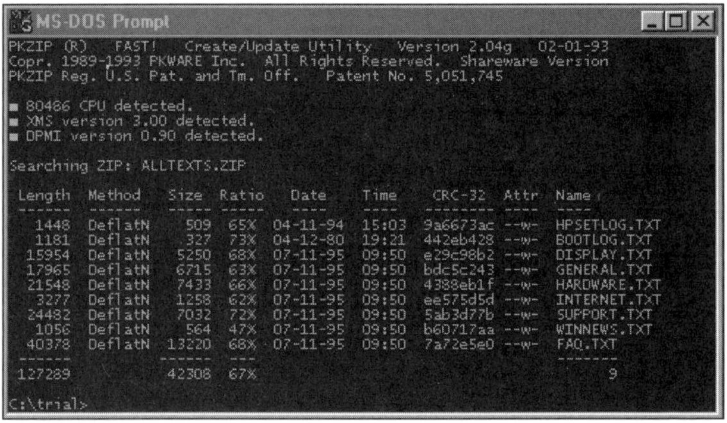

Figure 8.4 *The -v option lists the contents of an archive.*

As you can see in the figure, -v by itself yields quite a hefty report. Imagine what it would look like if there were dozens of files in the archive. You can control the report's contents by adding to -v the parameters shown in Table 8.1.

Table 8.1 Parameters for the -v Option

Parameter	Effect
b	Displays a *briefer* report.
c	Displays *comments* in addition to the other information.
m	Displays one page at a time; you press a key when you're ready to see *more*.
r	Lists the files in *reverse* order.
t	Displays *technical* information about each file in the archive.

Only one of the following characters may be specified per command:

d	Sorts the list by *date* and time.
e	Sorts the list by filename *extension*.

n	Sorts the list by *name*.
o	Sorts the list in its natural *order*—the order of the files in the archive.
p	Sorts the list by *percentage*.
s	Sorts the list by file *size*.

You combine parameters to create the report that you want. For example, suppose that you want to see a brief report with comments, sorted in reverse order by date and time, one page at a time. The correct option would be -vbcrdm.

You'll find the m parameter especially helpful because it prevents the first part of the report from scrolling off the screen before you get a chance to read it.

T I P

Unzipping Files into the Current Directory

Now let's suppose that you want to unzip **alltexts.zip** into the current directory. If you want to extract all the files, any of these commands would do:

```
pkunzip alltexts. *.*

pkunzip alltexts

pkunzjr alltexts
```

The first two commands have exactly the same effect. But the third calls on PKUnzip Junior, which is a smaller and faster program with limited capabilities.

If you have a really fast computer—say a Pentium 100 or faster—you probably won't notice any difference in speed between PKUnzip and PKUnzip Junior.

N O T E

Figure 8.5 shows an example of a report from PKUnzip Junior. As you can see, it lists all the files that were unzipped.

Figure 8.5 *This report shows files unzipped by PKUnzip Junior.*

PKUnzip Junior can handle up to 512 files. If you try to unzip an archive that contains more than 512 files, you'll see the message "Too many files." You can still extract the archive with PKUnzip.

NOTE

UNZIPPING TO A DIFFERENT DIRECTORY

When you want to unzip to a different directory, you must use a command with this general syntax:

```
pkunzip [options] archive directory [files]
```

```
pkunzjr [option] archive directory\
```

For example, the following command unzips the entire archive to the directory named **\savedocs\texts**:

```
pkunzjr alltexts \savedocs\texts\
```

With PKUnzip Junior, it's important to put the backslash at the end of the pathname; otherwise, you'll get erroneous results. But the backslash is optional with PKUnzip.

TIP

PARTIAL EXTRACTIONS

To extract just some of the files from an archive, you must use PKUnzip because PKUnzip Junior unzips entire archives only. As with PKZip, you place the names of the desired files after the archive's name, as in this example:

```
pkunzip alltexts doc*.txt tips.txt
```

To place them in a different directory, you must specify the directory name as a separate parameter before the filenames. The following command unzips only the specified files to the target directory. The space after the directory name is important. Without it, the command would have a different effect, which could result in an error message.

```
pkunzip alltexts \savedocs\text doc*.txt tips.txt
```

You can specify only one target directory per command. You must use a series of commands if you want to unzip files to several directories.

NOTE

Like PKZip, PKUnzip won't warn you if some of the files aren't found. It only warns you if *no* files were found.

OVERWRITING FILES

If PKUnzip or PKUnzip Junior finds an existing file with the same name as the one it is trying to unzip, it displays this message: "Warning! *filename* already exists. Overwrite (y/n/a/r)? " Type **Y** for *yes* or **N** for *no*. Figure 8.6 shows an example where I overwrote some files but not others. Notice that when I typed **Y**, PKUnzip Junior unzipped (inflated) the file. But when I typed **N**, PKUnzip Junior skipped the file and asked about the next one.

Figure 8.6 *By default, PKUnzip and Junior ask for permission to overwrite files.*

You can also type **A**, for *all*, if you want PKUnzip to finish the job without asking you about overwriting any more. It automatically overwrites the rest of the files. Another option is **R**, for *rename*, which gives you the chance to rename the file to be unzipped so that it won't overwrite the existing file. When you type **R**, PKUnzip asks "New name?" on the next line. You type a filename and press **Enter** to continue.

If you know in advance that some files in the directory might be overwritten, you can use the -o option on the command line to avoid being asked about overwriting. Specify -o to always overwrite existing files or -o- to never overwrite existing files. You can use -o with both PKUnzip and PKUnzip Junior. (This is PKUnzip Junior's only option.) But -o- works with PKUnzip only.

UNZIPPING SELF-EXTRACTING ARCHIVES

A self-extracting archive is actually a program—its extension is .exe—that duplicates many of the functions of PKUnzip or PKUnzip Junior. It's meant for people who don't have a separate unzipping program and/or don't know how to use one. But now that you know how to use PKUnzip and PKUnzip Junior, you have much more control over self-extracting archives too, because you can access them with the PKUnzip command with all its options. For example, suppose that you want to see the contents of a self-extracting archive named **gestures.exe**—just to make sure that it really is a self-extracting archive and not a trojan horse:

```
pkunzip -vb gestures.exe
```

A *trojan horse* is a program—often harmful—that pretends to be a different program. Trojan horses are discussed in more detail in Chapter 13.

NOTE

You have to include the extension **.exe** or PKUnzip will look for an archive named **gestures.zip**.

TIP

Of course, you can extract the entire archive to the current directory by just entering its filename as a command, like this:

```
gestures
```

And you can select files to extract by including their names in the command, like this:

```
gestures doc*.txt tips.txt
```

Suppose that you want to unzip all the files to the directory named **\docs\backtext**. Here is the command you would use:

```
gestures \docs\backtext\
```

To unzip specific files to a different directory:

```
gestures \docs\backtext\ doc*.txt tips.txt
```

If the file is a junior self-extracting archive, you won't be able to extract specific files from it by running the self-extractor itself. Figure 8.7 shows what happens when you try. The junior self-extractor thinks the filename is a directory name and tries to use it as the path for the first file in the archive—hence, the strange message, "Can't create: tips.txtHPSETLOG.TXT." Your real clue that you're dealing with a junior self-extractor is up in the first line of the report, where it says "Mini Self Extract Utility." That word *Mini* means junior. To solve the problem, either extract all the files or use PKUnzip to extract specific files.

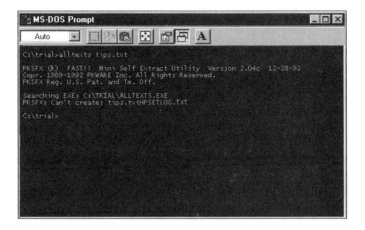

Figure 8.7 *Trying to extract specific files from a junior self-extracting archive produces this cryptic message.*

If the self-extractor finds an existing file of the same name as the file to be unzipped, it displays this message: "Warning! Filename already exists. Overwrite (y/n)?" Notice that only two options are offered—yes and no. But all four options work; you can use *A* for *all* or *R* for *rename*, even though they are not mentioned.

CREATING SELF-EXTRACTING ARCHIVES

Creating a self-extracting archive is fairly simple. All you need is a command like this:

```
zip2exe alltexts
```

Zip2exe responds with this message:

```
° Creating a Full Featured Self Extractor
ALLTEXTS.ZIP => ALLTEXTS.EXE
```

To create a junior self-extracting archive, which is much smaller, add the -j option like this:

```
zip2exe -j alltexts
```

Zip2exe displays this response:

```
° Creating a Junior Self Extractor
ALLTEXTS.ZIP => ALLTEXTS.EXE
```

INTERRUPTING JOBS

What if you realize that you typed the wrong command after you press the **Enter** key, and the command is already processing? You can interrupt any job by pressing **Ctrl+C**. This kills the job and returns you to the command prompt. If a new archive was being created, it is eliminated. But if files were being added to, deleted from, or extracted from an existing archive, any files already finished remain.

BEYOND THE BASICS

Now let's take a look at some of the more advanced tasks that you can accomplish with the PKZip family, such as adding comments and encrypting.

PKZip's Options

Table 8.2 summarizes all PKZip's options. There's no such summary in the software manual, so you'll find this table a handy reference tool!

NOTE

You can display an option summary on your monitor with the -h (help) options, but the list is complicated and hard to read, in my opinion. I think my list is much clearer.

Table 8.2 PKZip Command Option Summary

Adding, Updating, and Deleting Files

-v	View file information*
-d	Delete specified files*
-x	Exclude specified files*
-e	Specify compression level*
-m	Move files (delete originals after zipping)*
-u	Update files*
-f	Freshen (update indicated files only)*
-s	Encrypt files*
-r	Recurse subdirectories#
@	Specify list file#
-@	Generate list file#
-&	Span multiple disks#
-w	Add hidden and system files#
-j	Mask specified file attributes#

Managing Backups

-a+	Turn off archive attributes of added files#
-i	Add files with positive archive attributes, turn archive attributes off#
-i-	Add files with positive archive attributes, don't turn archive attributes off#
-t	Select files older than specified date#
-T	Select files younger than specified date#

Adding and Managing Comments

-c	Add/edit comments for each archived file*
-ac	Add/edit comments for all updated files*
-z	Add comment to archive itself*
-q	Enable ANSI control codes in comments#
-q-	Disable ANSI control codes in comments#

Including Pathnames

-p	Preserve specified pathnames#
-rp	Recurse subdirectories and preserve structure below #

Managing Date of Archive

-k	Don't update date of archive#
-k-	Set archive date to current date#
-o	Set archive date to date of latest file in archive#
-o-	Set archive date to current date#

Miscellaneous Functions

-b	Create temporary archive on specified drive/directory#
-h	Display help (command summary)#
-l	Display license agreement#
-!	Include Authenticity Verification Information#
-$	Store volume label as part of archive#
-=	Open file in compatibility mode#

*Covered in this chapter

#Not covered in this chapter

Excluding Files

Because you're limited to 127 characters in DOS commands, you sometimes have to be pretty clever to include in one command all the files you want. Sometimes the easiest solution is to exclude the files you don't want instead. For example, the following command adds all the files in the current directory except those with **.tmp** or **.bak** extensions:

```
pkzip -x*.tmp -x*.bak collect.zip
```

As you can see, you can specify several -x options in one command. You can also use a combination of includes and excludes to accomplish your goal. The following command includes all **.txt** and **.rtf** files except **doc*.txt** and **doc*.rtf**.

```
pkzip -xdoc*.txt -xdoc*.rtf alltexts *.txt *.rtf
```

Selecting a Compression Level

You can use the -e option to specify the level of compression for a job. A parameter goes with -e to indicate the desired level of compression, as shown in Table 8.3. For example, if you want to request maximum compression for a job, you might enter this command:

```
pkzip -ex alltexts
```

Table 8.3 PKZip Compression Levels

Parameter	Method	Sample Compression Ratio*
x	Maximum compression—takes the longest to compress but produces the smallest files	68%
n	Normal compression (the default level)—a balance between speed and size	68%
f	Fast compression—takes less time to compress than the normal level but produces a larger file	66%
s	Superfast compression—takes even less time but yields a larger file	62%
0	Zero compression—for archiving files already compressed	0%

*The sample compression ratios are based on an ASCII text file.

NOTE

Because -en is usually the default, you would never need to specify -en for normal compression unless you have configured your PKZip to use a different default.

Suppose that you're zipping up a bunch of GIFs to email to a friend. GIFs are already compressed, and there's no use watching PKZip spin its wheels trying to compress them further. So you might request zero compression with this command:

```
pkzip -e0 photos *.gif
```

In PKZip's reports, you'll see the word "storing" rather than "deflating" for files with zero compression.

Moving Files

Usually, PKZip leaves the original file alone, creating a copy to compress and archive. But if you want to move files into the archive instead of merely copying them, include the -m option, which has no parameters. The following command archives all the .doc files in the current directory and then deletes the originals:

```
pkzip -m olddocs *.doc
```

Updating and Freshening an Archive

Suppose that you zipped a complete report a couple of days ago—chapter files plus accompanying spreadsheets, charts, and illustrations—say a hundred files altogether. Now you have modified several chapters and a couple spreadsheets, and you want to update the archive with the modified files. One way to do it is to spell out the names of the files you want to add to the document, like this:

```
pkzip report chap01.doc chap04.doc chap07.doc chap18.doc
forecst4.wks forecst7.wks
```

PKZip will automatically replace any files in the archive with the same names as these files. But what if you don't remember all the files that you have changed? Or what if you want to be extra sure that you include all modifications in the archive before you email it to your client? Another way to bring the archive up to date is with the *freshen* option, like this:

```
pkzip -f report
```

This command causes PKZip to compare the archive to the source directory. When it finds a file in the archive with the same name as a source file, it compares their dates and times. If the source file is newer, PKZip replaces the archived file with the newer one. In this way, PKZip locates all the modified files for you. With the -f option, you don't have to spell out the names of the files to be updated.

Now suppose that you also added three new illustrations to the report and you need to add them to the archive too. The -f option won't pick them up because their names don't match any files currently in the archive. But the -u (update) option adds both modified and new files to the archive, so this command will do the job:

```
pkzip -u report
```

T I P

Many people get confused by freshen (-f) and update (-u), but the difference is simple. Freshen adds modified files only, whereas update adds new and modified files.

You can include filenames with the freshen or update option to limit the files that are considered. The following command, for example, freshens only the **.doc** files in the archive:

```
pkzip -f report *.doc
```

Adding Comments to an Archive

PKZip's comment feature lets you add remarks to an archive. Comments can be used to tell your recipients (and remind yourself) about the files in the archive. You can add an overall comment for the archive itself and comments for each of its files.

Suppose that you are creating a new archive and want to include comments in it. You would use the -z option to add a comment for the archive itself, but which option do you use to add comments for the files? Because you want to add files *and* add comments, you use -ac:

```
pkzip -z -ac report
```

As soon as it creates the archive, PKZip asks: "Zip comment?" You can type a comment up to 127 characters long. When you press **Enter**, PKZip stores the comment in the file and starts adding files. For each file it asks:

```
Adding:CHAP01.DOC        Deflating  (68%), done
Comment?
```

For each file, you can type a comment up to 59 characters.

Now that you know about comments, you might want to add them to your existing archives. If you just want to add comments without adding any files, use -c instead of -ac. You'll need -z too if you want to add a comment for the archive itself. If you also include filenames in the command, only those files are displayed for comments, which can save you a lot of time in a long archive. The files themselves are not updated; -c suppresses the addition of new or updated files and merely lets you work on the comments.

Any time that you want to review and edit the comments in an archive, use -z and -c again. PKZip will display the comments for the specified files and give you a chance to change them.

Suppose that you want to add some new files to the archive and comments, and you want to review and edit all existing comments. You'll need to use -ac rather than -c. The -ac option lets you add files, and it also reviews all the comments in the archive.

But what if you don't want to review existing comments, just add them for the new files? You need to use -C (uppercase C) rather than -ac. With -C, you only add comments for new additions to the archive. Even freshened files keep their old comments.

Don't forget that each comment you add increases the size of the archive. Comments are not compressed, so if you add a 127-character comment, you increase the file size by 127 characters.

T I P

Okay, now you've got comments in your archive, but how does your recipient see them? The only way is to use PKZip with the -vc option. PKUnzip and PKUnzip Junior do not have a similar option, nor are comments displayed automatically during unzipping, not even with a self-extracting archive. This is unfortunate because your recipient might not be aware of the comments and might never see them.

Encrypting Files

The Internet is not a very safe place for sensitive information. Not only is it much too easy to mistype one character in an email address and send a file to the wrong person, there might also be people actually intercepting your email to pick up confidential information without your knowledge. If all you send are photos of your kids, recipes for your grandmother's cookies, and the chapters of your latest book, you probably don't have much to worry about. (Unless your child is the heir to a throne, your grandmother is Mrs. Fields, or your latest book is the sequel to *The Stand*.) But if you're transmitting the designs for your spring catalog, your corporate downsizing plan, or the president's x-rays, then you would be wise to be cautious.

PKZip can encrypt a file so that no one can read it without the correct password. Anyone who unzips it without the password will see nothing but nonsense. Use the -s option to encrypt the files that you're adding to the archive. You can include a password in the -s option, as in -sLandRover#441. If you omit the password in the option, PKZip will ask for it when it starts to add the files.

When unzipping, the password must be included in the -s option. To unzip and decrypt the files, your recipient would enter a command like this:

```
pkunzip -sLandRover#441 report
```

N O T E   How do you communicate the password to your recipient? That's a separate problem. If your email is vulnerable, you can't email it. But wouldn't your phone calls, telegrams, and surface letters be just as vulnerable? I'll leave this one up to you to solve.

There are a few rules you must follow in creating a good password:

- If you include the password in the -s option, its length is limited only by the length of the command itself, which can't be longer than 127 characters.
- If it includes spaces, you must enclose it in quotes, as in "Five #10 pencils."

- Passwords are case-sensitive. When unzipping an encrypted file, you must use exactly the same characters and case that you used when creating the file. "BubbleGum" is not the same password as "bubblegum" or "Bubblegum."

If your password is good enough, no one will be able to decrypt your file no matter how expert he or she is nor what "hacker" program is used. But that's a very big "if," because most people choose weak passwords that are easy to remember. If you want to create an unbreakable password, follow these guidelines:

- Use at least eight characters, preferably more (the longer it is, the harder it is to crack).
- Include some uppercase letters, some lowercase letters, some digits, and some symbols. Most people make the mistake of using just words, and those are the easiest passwords to crack with hacker programs.
- Don't use any words or expressions associated with you. For example, don't use your name or the name of a relative, pet, favorite performer, athlete, and so on. Don't use your social security number, birth date, telephone number, checking account number, or any other number related to you. Don't use a "favorite" object: food, movie, sports team, television program, and so on. Don't use your hometown, your street, your college, your high school, and so on. Don't use the name of an object that you can see while sitting at your computer.

- If you must use whole words, use ones that have no association with you, such as *field*, *cardboard*, *purple*, *thousand*, or *flange*. But it's better not to use a single word as a password; use a sentence or phrase instead.

Here are some examples of good passwords:

Thomas Jefferson 1801-1809

(Five * Ten) + Two = 52

3 Large Red+White+Blue Flags

Remember your password! If you forget it, you are out of luck. There is no way to recover it and no way to decrypt the file without it. Not even PKWare can decrypt it or recover your password because the information is not stored in the archive.

By the way, encryption is on a file-by-file basis. One archive might have some unencrypted files as well as files encrypted under several different passwords. Each time you add files to the archive, you can use a different password if you want. When recipients want to unzip the files, they might have to use several PKUnzip commands so that they can enter all the various passwords.

PKUnzip's Options

PKUnzip doesn't have nearly as many options as PKZip. As you can see in Table 8.4, you already know some of them. You know how to view file information, provide a password, control the overwriting of existing files, and exclude files from being unzipped. In this section, you'll learn the difference between the freshen and newer options and how to test an archive's integrity.

Table 8.4 PKUnzip Command Option Summary

Option	Effect
-f	Freshen target directory*
-n	Extract newer files only*
-o	Overwrite existing files*
-x	Exclude specified files from extraction*
-t	Test archive integrity*
-s	Decrypt using specified password*
-v	View file information*
-c	Extract to console#
-d	Restore directory structure#
-e	Extract in specified order#
-h	Display help#
-j	Mask specified attributes#
-l	Display license agreement#
-p	Extract to the printer#
-q	Enable ANSI comments#
-$	Restore volume label#
-@	Generate list file#
@	Use list file#

UPDATING THE TARGET DIRECTORY

The freshen (-f) and newer (-n) options are the inverses of
PKZip's freshen and update options. Both options cause PKUnzip
to compare the files in the archive to the files in the target
directory (limited by any filenames included in the command).
With freshen, only existing files are replaced by newer ones from
the archive. With newer, newer files replace existing files and any
new files are extracted to the target directory.

TESTING THE INTEGRITY OF AN ARCHIVE

By now you know that files can get damaged as they travel the Internet. By the time you download an archive, it might have been corrupted so that, when you unzip it, you get wrong data in some of the files. You can test the files in an archive with the -t option. PKUnzip checks each of the specified files, or all the files if you don't specify any, and displays a report like this:

```
Testing: TEST.TXT       OK
Testing: HPSETLOG.TXT   OK
Testing: BOOTLOG.TXT    OK
Testing: DISPLAY.TXT    OK
```

If a file appears to be corrupted, you'll see a message like this:

```
Testing: TEST.TXT  PKUNZIP: (W15) Warning! file fails CRC check
```

That message might scroll off your screen if it occurs near the beginning of the archive. But at the end of the job, you'll also see the following message, so you'll know that some problems were encountered:

```
ALLTEXTS.ZIP has errors!
```

About the only way to fix the error is to redownload the archive. If it comes from a Web or ftp site, download it again. If it still has errors, contact the person in charge of the site and ask him or her to replace the stored file. If the problem archive was emailed to you, ask the sender to email it again.

How does PKUnzip know that a file is corrupted, and what is a CRC check? When a file is archived by PKZip or a similar program, the zipper adds together all the data in the unzipped file as if it were numeric data. (It doesn't matter if it isn't numeric data, the process works anyway.) It manipulates the result to come up with a number called a *Cyclic Redundancy Check* (CRC). It stores the CRC value with the file in the archive. When you test the file, PKUnzip unzips it into memory (but doesn't store the result on disk) and recalculates the CRC. If it gets a different CRC, it knows that the data must have been changed after it was zipped, and therefore the file is corrupted. If it gets the same CRC, the odds are extremely high that the data is the same data that was zipped.

You'll see the CRC when you view information unless you request a brief report. It's just a meaningless value, so you can safely ignore it.

T I P

OPTIONS FOR SELF-EXTRACTING ARCHIVES

A full-featured self-extracting file offers many of the same options as PKUnzip, as shown in Table 8.5. These are the same options as PKUnzip's, so you already know how to use them, and I won't discuss them further here. A junior self-extractor, as mentioned earlier, offers only the -o option.

Table 8.5 Self-Extracting Archive Command Option Summary

Option	Effect
-o	Overwrite existing files
-n	Extract only newer files
-t	Test file integrity
-s	Decrypt with specified password
-d	Re-create directories
-c	Extract to console
-p	Extract to printer
-l	Display license agreement
@	Use list file

Don't forget that you can also use PKUnzip itself on a self-extracting archive, junior or full-featured, so that you can apply the full range of PKUnzip's options to it. All you have to do is include the self-extractor's name in the PKUnzip command, like this:

```
pkunzip -vbm gestures.exe
```

USING PKZIPFIX

Certain kinds of problems are correctable without redownloading the file. Sometimes the archive information at the beginning of the file—PKZip's headers and the directory of files in the archive—gets damaged en route. In such cases, the program called PKZipFix might be able to fix the archive. If one of your unzipping programs encounters problems in the archive information, it will display a message to run PKZipFix.

 TIP Anytime you accidentally try to unzip a file that isn't an archive, you'll see the suggestion to run PKZipFix. That's because the unzipper can't find PKZip's normal archive information at the beginning of the file and thinks the archive is corrupted. Just ignore the suggestion and correct your original command to unzip the right file.

It's simple to run PKZipFix, which has no options. Here's an example:

```
pkzipfix alltexts.zip
```

PKZipFix produces a file called **zipfixed.zip**, which you might not be able to unzip. If you can unzip it, it might not contain all the files of the original archive. But sometimes half a loaf is better than none. In most cases, though, if PKZipFix doesn't completely repair the file, you're best off redownloading the file.

USING PKZIP'S MANUAL

Look in your PKWare directory for a file called **manual.doc**. That's the documentation for your PKZip family software. It's an ASCII text file, but it doesn't look very good when you open it in a Windows editor such as WordPad or Write. Your best bet is to use the DOS editor to view and/or print it. In your DOS window, enter the following command to open the file:

```
edit c:\pkware\manual.doc
```

Now you can use the EDIT's Search command to find a topic.

I find the manual too hard to work with on my monitor. The table of contents (at the front) and index (at the back) refer to page numbers that I have trouble finding. So I printed the whole thing—around 130 pages—punched holes in it, added divider tabs, and stuck it in a binder. I find it much easier to work with this way. So much for the paperless office.

The manual includes a section documenting the options for each of the PKZip family programs. Even the two programs not included with the shareware version are described in the manual. A Troubleshooting section, a Frequently Asked Questions (FAQ) section, and a complete list of error and warning messages with explanations are also included.

The shareware version of the manual that's included in the book is missing a couple of sections: the tutorial and the explanation of how PKZip compresses data. This helps to keep the manual small enough to fit on the disk, and it takes less time for people to download from bulletin boards. When you register your copy of PKZip, you'll receive the full manual.

WHAT'S NEXT?

In the next chapter, you'll enter the somewhat mysterious world of Macintosh compression. Mac users everywhere use a format called StuffIt, pioneered by Raymond Lau, and we'll look at what to do if you run into these files. We'll also look at another utility that easily handles these files and can even handle other formats as well.

CHAPTER 9

Using StuffIt Expander

It happened to me only last week—a Macintosh user sent to a group of friends some files that he had compressed with the Macintosh standard compression tool, StuffIt. Letters were flying back and forth among the PC users, "What do I do with these things?" Meanwhile, the Macintosh users were sitting back and winking at each other.

As a PC user, you don't have to wonder how to handle a .sit file. With StuffIt Expander, you can unstuff that file before your Macintosh buddies have a chance for a chuckle or a wink. As its name implies, StuffIt Expander only expands, it doesn't compress. I don't think that you need to create .sit files for your Mac friends. Their StuffIt software can unzip .zip files just as easily as .sit files, so why bother cluttering up your hard drive with unnecessary software?

WHAT STUFFIT EXPANDER CAN DO

I chose to show you StuffIt Expander because it can do one thing that none of the other programs in this book can do: it can unstuff files in StuffIt (.sit) format. Even though .sit files are used mostly with the Macintosh, you might occasionally receive one and need to unstuff it. Many Macintosh users on the Internet don't realize that PC users don't normally deal with .sit files. So when they want to send you something, they just naturally stuff it. I have one Macintosh friend who just naturally tries to unstuff everything I send her. Every time I tried to send her a file, she complained that she couldn't open it. When I finally realized that she was trying to open it in StuffIt, I suggested she use her word processor instead. It worked perfectly in her word processor. (I'm telling you this rather long story because you might run into a similar problem with a Macintosh friend.)

But that's not all StuffIt Expander can do. Table 9.1 shows all the formats it can expand and decode. There's some overlap between StuffIt Expander and the other software discussed in this book, especially WinZip, because every program wants to be your only compression or encoding utility. But I find that it takes a combination of programs to fully cover all the formats you're going to run into on the Internet.

Table 9.1 Compression and Encoding Formats Handled by StuffIt Expander

Format	Extension	Also handled by...
Archives		
StuffIt	.sit	none
PKZip	.zip	PKZip, WinZip
arj	.arj	none*
arc	.arc	none*
gzip	.gz, .z	WinZip
Self-Extracting Archives		
StuffIt	.sea	none
PKZip	.exe	PKZip, WinZip
arj	.exe	none*

Encoded

uuencode	.uue	WinZip, Funduc
BinHex	.hqx	WinZip, Funduc

Combinations

StuffIt and BinHex	.sit.hqx	none
tar and gzip	tar.gz, tar.z, .tgz, .taz	WinZip

*Although WinZip provides an interface for handling these file types, it does not actually expand them unless you have extra software.

The folks at Aladdin have tried to make StuffIt Expander as simple as possible. Its window, which you can see in Figure 9.1, is easy to use. But most of the time, you don't even need the window. You just double-click a file to expand or decode it. Or you can minimize the window and drag and drop files on it.

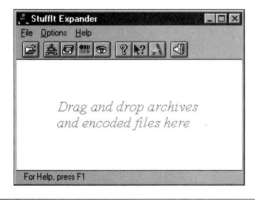

Figure 9.1 *StuffIt Expander's window is easy to use, but often not even necessary.*

Because the StuffIt Expander window was designed to be used in the minimized state, its control menu is extended to include several more options when it is minimized. The control menu is the menu that pops up when you click a minimized window or, in Windows 95 and higher, right-click the **Taskbar** button. It usually contains options to restore or maximize the window. With StuffIt Expander, it also contains options to expand a file, stay on top (so that you can find it easily on a cluttered desktop), reset your options, and access the help library.

Another unique feature lets you designate a directory as a *watch directory*. StuffIt Expander checks this directory every few minutes and, if it finds any files it can handle, extracts or decodes them without being asked. So if you always use the same directory to download files, you can pretty much automate your decoding and extracting tasks.

There are a few things you can't do with StuffIt Expander. You can't select files from an archive; it always extracts the entire archive. You can't extract encrypted or segmented archives. And of course, because it's just an expander, you can't zip, stuff, or encode.

INSTALLING STUFFIT EXPANDER

I couldn't fit everything on the book's disk, so I had to leave StuffIt Expander out. But you shouldn't have any trouble finding it. It's freeware, and it's available everywhere. You can download it from Aladdin System's FTP site, at **ftp://ftp.aladdinsys.com**. You can also get it from America Online (keyword ALADDIN), CompuServe, and probably your local BBS as well. Look for the file named **sitex10.exe**, which is the installer for the Windows version of StuffIt Expander. (Be sure to get the version for Windows.) As of right now, there's no 32-bit version, but the 16-bit version works fine with Windows 95 and higher.

After you download **sitex10.exe**, you run it to start the installer. Run it just as you would any other Windows application. For example, you could double-click it in Windows 3.1 File Manager or Windows 95 Explorer. When you run it, you'll see the window shown in Figure 9.2. All you have to do is fill out this form and click **Install**.

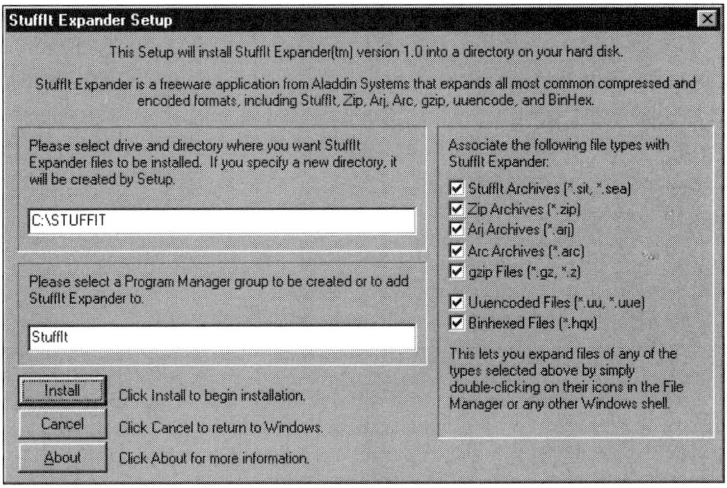

Figure 9.2 *The StuffIt Expander installer gathers all the information it needs in one window.*

At the upper left, you indicate where to install StuffIt Expander. The suggested directory is **c:\stuffit,** but you can change that if you want. The installer will create the desired directory if it doesn't already exist.

Next, you indicate where the StuffIt Expander's program icon should be placed. In Windows 3.*x*, you designate a program group. For Windows 95 and higher, you designate a folder on the Start menu. The suggested group is named

StuffIt, but you can change that if you want. The installer will create the desired group if it doesn't already exist.

On the right side of the window, you select the file types that you want to associate with StuffIt Expander. Associating a file type with a program makes it easy to run the program by opening the file. For example, if you associate zip archives with StuffIt Expander, whenever you double-click (or otherwise open) a **.zip** file, StuffIt Expander starts up automatically to process it.

T I P   I prefer to use WinZip's more extensive facilities and Funduc's shell extensions for the files they handle, so I don't keep all the associations suggested in this window. I uncheck the boxes for zip archives, gzip files, Uuencoded files, and binhexed files. But I retain the associations for StuffIt, Arj, and Arc archives.

After you have specified everything that you want to install, click the **Install** button to continue. It only takes the installer a few seconds to finish the installation.

EXPANDING AND DECODING FILES

There are several ways to unstuff or decode a file:

- You can use the **File|Expand** command in the open StuffIt Expander window. This opens a browse dialog box where you can select the desired file.

- You can drop one or more files on the StuffIt Expander window while it's open.

You can process several files at once this way.

T I P

- You can drop one or more files on the StuffIt Expander window while it's minimized.

This method doesn't work in Windows 95 and higher because you can't drop a file on a Taskbar button. But if you pause the file(s) over the Taskbar button for a few moments, the window will restore itself automatically and then you can drop the file(s) on the open window.

N O T E

- When the StuffIt Expander window is minimized, you can click it once to pop up its extended control menu and then choose **Expand** from the control menu to open a browse dialog box where you can select a file.

For Windows 95 and higher, right-click the StuffIt Expander button in the Taskbar to pop up the extended control menu.

T I P

- For files associated with StuffIt Expander, you can double-click or otherwise open the file in a program like Windows 3.*x* File Manager or Windows 95 Explorer.

No matter how you start the process, you'll see a progress box like the one shown in Figure 9.3. And that's it—no questions to answer, no choices to make. But you don't get any choices about what was expanded or decoded or where it was placed. You have to make those choices in advance, by setting the StuffIt Expander options, which are discussed next.

Figure 9.3 StuffIt Expander displays a progress box while expanding or decoding a file.

StuffIt Expander Options

So where does StuffIt Expander put the unstuffed and decoded files? That depends on what options you set. StuffIt Expander has four categories of options: Expansion, Destination, Cross Platform, and Watch Directory. You can access the Options dialog box, shown in Figure 9.4, by selecting any one of these categories from the **Options** menu or by selecting **Options** from the extended control menu when the window is minimized.

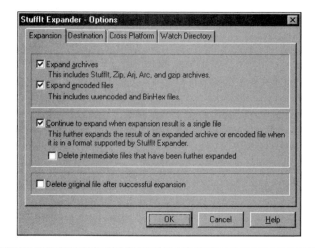

Figure 9.4 StuffIt Expander's Options dialog box includes four pages of options.

THE EXPANSION OPTIONS

Figure 9.4 shows the expansion options, which control how StuffIt Expander expands and decodes files. In the top section, you can turn off expansion or decoding if you want. (I don't know why they refer to "expansion" of uuencode and BinHex files. Maybe they don't want to confuse us by introducing the term "decoding.")

The option in the middle section controls what happens when StuffIt Expander expands or decodes a file only to find that it contains another compressed or encoded file, as with a **.sit.hqx** file or a **.zip** file inside a **.uue** file. With this option enabled—meaning that it has a check mark—StuffIt Expander will expand or decode the enclosed file too. Without the check mark, it stops after expanding the containing file.

NOTE   No matter how this option is set, StuffIt Expander won't automatically expand multiple compressed and encoded files contained within another one. Just today, I unstuffed a file that turned out to contained several zip archives. I had to expand each **.zip** file individually. (You often find **.zip** files inside other **.zip** archives, but this is the first time I ever saw **.zip** files inside a **.sit** file.)

If you enable the **Continue to expand...** option, you can also request that intermediate files be deleted automatically. When StuffIt Expander decodes **controls.uue** to find **controls.zip**, which it then unzips, **controls.zip** is an intermediate file. You might feel that it's not necessary to keep intermediate files, as you can always process the outer file again to get back to the inner file. If so, consider checking this option, which is disabled by default.

The bottom option automatically deletes the original file after decoding or decompressing it. You pay your money and take your choice. Some people don't want a lot of compressed and encoded files sitting around on their hard drives. Others prefer to keep the original files for safety's sake and, in the case of shareware and freeware, so that they can pass them on to others if they like the software.

THE DESTINATION OPTIONS

The Destination options, shown in Figure 9.5, control where StuffIt Expander places the files that it extracts. By default, it creates a new directory with the same name as the archive under the original directory and puts the new files in there. For example, if it unzips a file in **c:\download** named **games.zip**, it creates a directory named **c:\download\games** for the unzipped files. If you don't like that method, you can tell StuffIt Expander to ask you for a destination directory every time it handles a file (**Ask Each time**), or you can name a destination directory that it should use every time (**Use**).

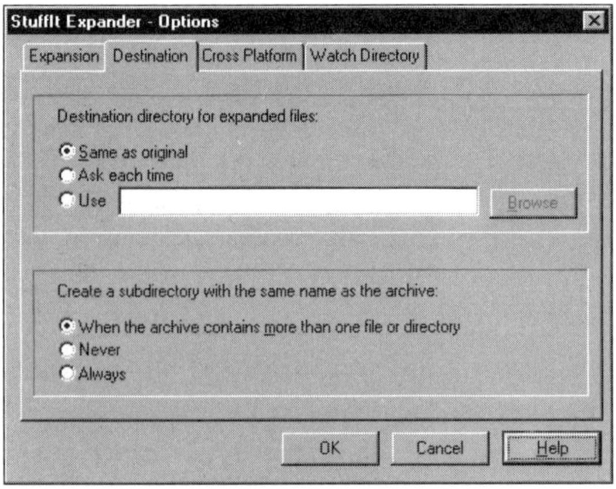

Figure 9.5 *The Destination option controls where the extracted files are placed.*

The bottom set of options determine whether StuffIt Expander creates a new directory to put the files in. By default, it does only if the archive contains multiple files. A single file goes into the same directory as the original archive. You can also choose to **Always** create a new directory, even in the case of a single file, or **Never** create a new directory.

FOR THE FUTURE

After you're comfortable with the basic StuffIt Expander functions, you might consider exploring the two advanced options: Watch Directory and Cross Platform. Watch Directory lets you set up a directory that StuffIt Expander will watch for files that it can handle (see Figure 9.6). Don't set up a watch directory casually—there are many considerations you must pay attention to. They are spelled out in StuffIt Expander's help library.

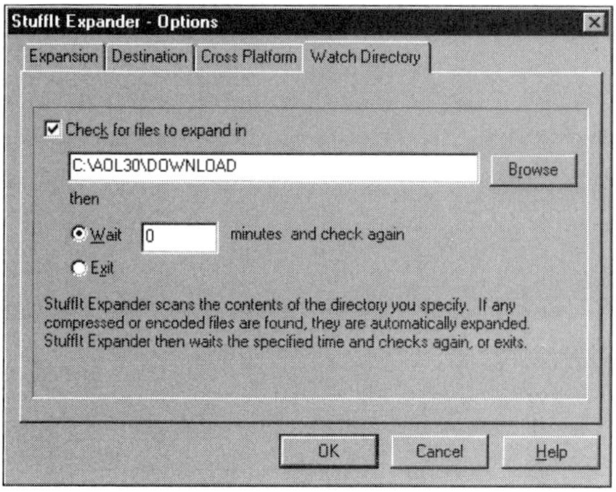

Figure 9.6 StuffIt Expander allows you to set up a Watch directory.

The Cross Platform options determine how StuffIt Expander handles Macintosh files that it decodes and decompresses on your PC. Here again, you'll need to do a lot of reading in the StuffIt Expander help library before deciding to change the default settings. Personally, I'm still using the defaults in this area, perhaps because I almost never download Macintosh files.

WHAT'S NEXT?

StuffIt Expander is only one of the decoders covered in this book. The next chapter shows you how to decode files with WinZip and the Funduc Shell Extensions.

CHAPTER 10

Decoding with WinZip and Decode Shell Extension

You've already learned how to unzip archives with WinZip in Chapter 7. The newest release of WinZip, version 6.2, also includes facilities for decoding MIME, uuencode, xxencode, and BinHex files. In addition, it can encode archives in uuencode format. (If you currently have release 6.1 or earlier, it's worth upgrading to 6.2 to get these encoding/decoding features.)

For Windows 95 and higher users (including NT), I have also included on the disk for this book a lovely little program called Decode Shell Extension, which lets you decode uuencode, xxencode, BinHex, and base64 (MIME) files right in Explorer. The shell extension is easy to install and use, as you'll see in this chapter.

What you'll learn in this chapter:

- How to decode files with WinZip
- How to encode files with WinZip
- How to install Funduc Decode Shell Extension
- How to decode files with Funduc Decode Shell Extension
- How to set file associations in Windows 3.*x* and Windows 95 and higher

DECODING WITH WINZIP

You start decoding with WinZip just like you start any other WinZip job:

- In WinZip Classic's window, choose **File|Open Archive** (**Ctrl+O**) or click the **Open** button and then select the encoded file in the browse dialog box.

WinZip shows you **.zip** files by default in the browse dialog box. Drop down the **type** list and choose **encoded files** to see them in the dialog box.

T I P

- Drag an encoded file from a shell program, such as File Manager or Explorer, and drop it on WinZip's window.
- In a shell program, drag an encoded file and drop it on WinZip's program icon.

Can you start WinZip's decoder simply by double-clicking (or otherwise opening) an encoded file? That depends on how your file types are associated with your various decoders. If **.uue** files are associated with WinZip on your system, for example, then double-clicking any **.uue** file will start up WinZip. But if they are associated with StuffIt Expander, double-clicking a **.uue** file will start up the expander instead.

The question of what is associated with what can be a hairy one. It depends on the order that you installed the various programs along with the installation options that you chose. At the end of this chapter, after you have learned about the Decode Shell Extension, I'll show you how to review and change your file associations so that you have the ultimate say-so in your own system.

N O T E

However you start the WinZip decoding job, the result is the same. You'll see the encoded file in the WinZip window. Select it and click **Extract** to decode it. Or, if the encoded file turns out to contain an archive, you'll see the message shown in Figure 10.1. When you click **Yes**, WinZip decodes the file and loads the archive into the window, just as if you had opened it. You can now extract the file as normal.

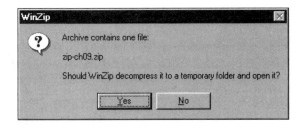

Figure 10.1 *You see this message when you open an encoded archive in WinZip.*

ENCODING WITH WINZIP

In the first part of this book, you learned that you must encode binary files before you post them in a Usenet newsgroup. You must also encode them for emailing if you don't have a MIME mailer. WinZip includes a uuencode feature that will do your encoding for you, but it will only encode files that have already been zipped.

How to encode an archive:

1. Open the archive in the WinZip window.
2. Choose **Actions|Uuencode** (**Ctrl+U**).

You'll see the message shown below.

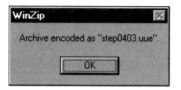

3. Click **OK** to finish the job.

The uuencoded file does not appear in the WinZip window at this point—the archive stays in the window. You have to specifically open the uuencoded file if you want to see it in the window.

WinZip puts the encoded file in the same directory as the original archive, so you shouldn't have any trouble finding it.

T I P

USING THE FUNDUC DECODE SHELL EXTENSION

The Decode Shell Extension from Funduc Software adds a **Decode** option to the context menu that pops up when you right-click a file in a Windows 95 or higher shell window, which includes the My Computer, Explorer, and Find windows and the browse dialog boxes. If the file is encoded with uuencode, xxencode, BinHex, or MIME, you can decode it simply by selecting the **Decode** option.

INSTALLING THE SHELL EXTENSION

I have included the freeware version of Decode Shell Extension, version 2.21, on the disk at the back of this book. Here's how to install it:

1. Insert the disk from the back of the book in drive A.
2. Start WinZip.
3. Open the file named **decext.zip** on drive A.
4. Click the **Install** button.

   The dialog box shown below appears:

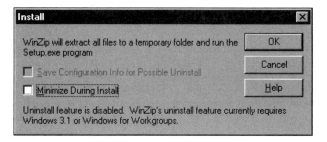

5. Click **OK**.

   The Decode Shell Extension installer starts up, and you'll see the first page of the Setup Wizard.

The first page asks you to make sure that Explorer is not running. This means that no shell windows should be open: Explorer, My Computer, Find, or a browse dialog box. Be sure to close all such windows before continuing.

NOTE

6. Click **Next** to continue.

   The next page of the wizard displays a readme file.
7. When you're finished reading the readme file, click **Next** to continue.

   The next page of the wizard lets you choose a directory for the shell extension.
8. Change the directory if you want. Then click **Next** to continue.

The next page of the wizard lets you choose a group folder for the shell extension. The determines where the shell extension will appear on your Start menu.

9. Change the group folder if you want. Then click **Next** to continue.

A message tells you that the shell extension was successfully installed.

10. Click **OK** to close the wizard.

You'll see a window with the two shell extension items: **Uninstall** and a readme file.

11. Read the readme file if you want. Then close the window.

12. Click **OK** to close the WinZip Install dialog box.

DECODING FILES WITH THE SHELL EXTENSION

Now you're ready to use the shell extension. When you want to decode a file, locate it in one of the shell windows and right-click it. A context menu pops up, similar to the one shown in Figure 10.2, with a **Decode** option.

*Figure 10.2 Decode Shell Extension adds a **Decode** option to Explorer's context menu.*

When you click **Decode**, you'll see the dialog box shown in Figure 10.3. Before you click **Yes**, be sure to notice the name and location of the newly decoded file. You don't have any choice about the name or location, but at least you can remember what they are. When you click **Yes**, the file is decoded, and you return to the shell.

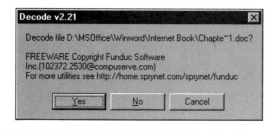

*Figure 10.3 You'll see this message when you click the **Decode** option.*

SETTING YOUR OWN FILE ASSOCIATIONS

Many of the programs in this book will make file associations so that you can start them up easily just by double-clicking a file. But each program you install might override some of the previous program's associations until you're not sure what's what. You can review and change your file associations at any time. This section will show you how.

By the way, these techniques work with any files that you want to associate with programs, not just your archives and encoded files. You could change the association of a **.doc** file or **.txt** file, for example.

CHANGING FILE ASSOCIATIONS IN WINDOWS 95 AND HIGHER

You review and change file associations in My Computer or Explorer. Here's how:

1. In the Explorer or My Computer window, choose **View|Options** to open the Options dialog box.

2. Click the **File Types** tab to open the dialog box shown below:

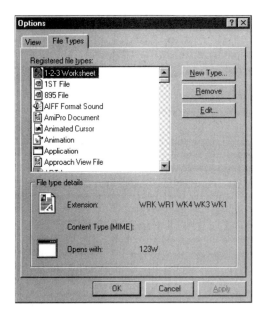

3. Scroll through the list of types until you find the type that you want to review and change.

4. Review the details in the **File Type Details** box and decide if you want to change them.

5. If you want to change them, click the **Edit** button to open the dialog box shown below.

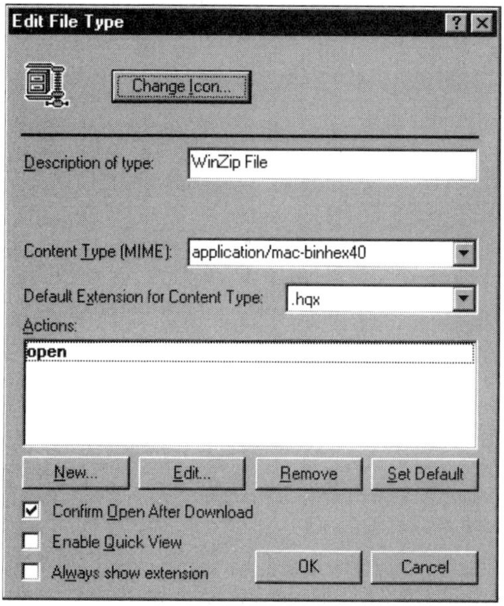

6. In the Actions box, click **Open** to select it.

7. Click **Edit** underneath the Actions box to open the dialog box shown below.

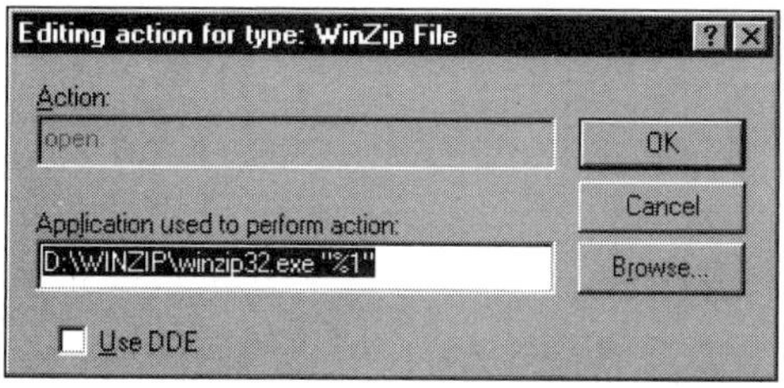

8. Click the **Browse** button and select the program that you want to associate with the file type.

9. Click **OK** or **Close** in each of the dialog boxes until you get back to the Options dialog box.

10. Repeat steps 3 through 9 until you have set all the associations that you want.

11. Click **Close** to close the Options dialog box.

   Your new associations should now work.

CHANGING FILE ASSOCIATIONS IN WINDOWS 3.x

You use File Manager to create file associations in Windows 3.x. Here's how:

1. Open File Manager.

2. Choose **File|Associate** to open the dialog box shown below.

3. Type the desired extension in the box labeled **Files With Extension**.

   The **Associate With** box scrolls to show the current association, if any.

4. If you want to change the association, scroll through the **Associate With** box and select another program.

T I P

If the desired program isn't in the **Associate With** box, click **Browse** to locate it.

5. Click **OK** to record the new association.

6. Repeat steps 2 through 5 as many times as you want to clean up your file associations.

Some Handy Internet Sites

You'll find the web site for Funduc Software at this address: http://home.sprynet.com/sprynet/funduc. You can download the latest version of Decode Shell Extension as well as other Funduc products here.

You'll find the WinZip site at http://winzip.com.

What's Next?

By now, you're pretty savvy about what to do when you receive a file named **chapters.zip, classes.uue,** or **sounds.sit.** But what if you get one named **report.y97**? The next chapter talks about what to do when you have no idea what type of file you're dealing with.

CHAPTER 11

What to Do If You're Not Sure

I have a friend who sends me files with names like **Shortsto.ry** and **Revision.1**. It drives me crazy, but no amount of begging has convinced her to use meaningful filename extensions. I guess her extensions are meaningful to her.

In my friend's case, I can call her and ask her whether she zipped the file, encoded it, what word processor she used, and so on. But sometimes you're faced with an unknown file type when you can't ask the person who sent or posted it. The extension might represent a perfectly legitimate file type that you just don't recognize, such as **.sdr** for a SmartDraw flowchart, **.ani** for a Windows animated cursor, or **.wmf** for Microsoft Works clipart.

This chapter shows you some techniques you can use to discover a file's type. What you'll learn in this chapter:

- How to look for an application's signature with an ASCII text editor
- Trying out an unknown file in a variety of applications
- How to use the power of the Internet to discover a file's type (and the software to view and edit it)

PROGRAM HEADERS AND TRAILERS

One of the first things you can try is peeking inside the file with an ASCII text editor. Many applications insert a header in front of each file and/or a trailer at the end that includes the name of the application. If you can open the file as ASCII text, even if most of the data is binary and unreadable, you might be able to spot the application name in the header or trailer. Of course, if the file really is an ASCII text file, you're home free.

Many ASCII text editors will display a file no matter what type of data it contains. I just did a little experiment and opened a zip file in DOS's EDIT, Windows 95's WordPad, and America Online's built-in text editor. I also opened it as a text file in a couple of word processors: Microsoft Word 7.0 and Microsoft Works 4.0. I failed to open it in Claris Works (couldn't recognize the file type), WordPerfect 6.0a (recognized the file type as incompatible), and Windows Notepad (file too long). I was able to open a shorter zip file in Notepad, however.

America Online's editor displayed only the first two characters of the file—it must have choked on the third character. However, the first two characters would have been enough because they were PK.

NOTE

Figure 11.1 shows what the zip file looks like in WordPad. As you can see, it's mostly binary junk, but the PK at the beginning gives you a clue that this is a zip file. You can also spot a filename in the first row, **FILEDONE.WAV**, one of the files the archive contains. Taking that as a cue, I searched for .WAV and found several other filenames mixed in among the binary data. That was just for fun because I already had enough information to know that it was a zip file.

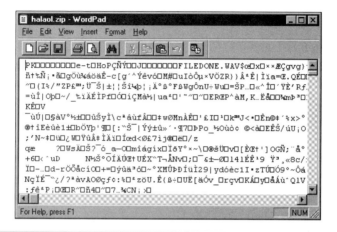

Figure 11.1 *The letters PK at the beginning of this file give you a clue that it's probably a zip file.*

Let's look at a few other file types. Figure 11.2 shows a MIME encoded file. Thanks to the standard MIME headers, there's no question about the file type in this case. Figure 11.3 shows a uuencoded file. The giveaway here is the first line, which contains "begin" followed by a three-digit number and a filename. And of course, uuencoded files always have a series of fixed-length lines starting with M, as explained in Chapter 2.

Figure 11.2 *The MIME headers tell you that this is a MIME-encoded file.*

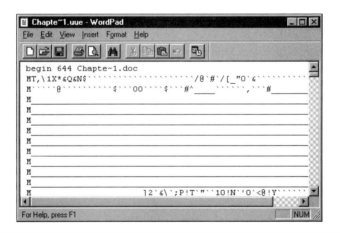

Figure 11.3 *The word "begin" and the lines starting with M are clues to a uuencoded file.*

Want to try your hand at identifying a few files? Figures 11.4 through 11.6 show three files for you to identify. The correct answers are given at the end of the chapter.

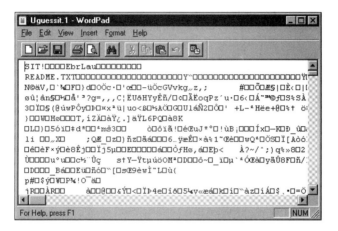

Figure 11.4 Can you figure out what type of file this is?

Figure 11.5 Here's another file for you to guess.

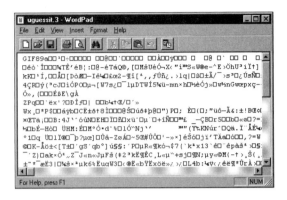

Figure 11.6 One more mystery file for you to guess.

If you can't find any clues at the beginning of the file, keep scrolling through. Figure 11.7 shows a **.doc** file created by Microsoft Word but displayed as a text file in Notepad. I had to scroll down quite a bit before I found the signature "Microsoft Word for Windows 95," which I have highlighted in the figure. (I had to use Notepad for this figure because WordPad displayed it as a Word document rather than ASCII text, so I couldn't see the signature.)

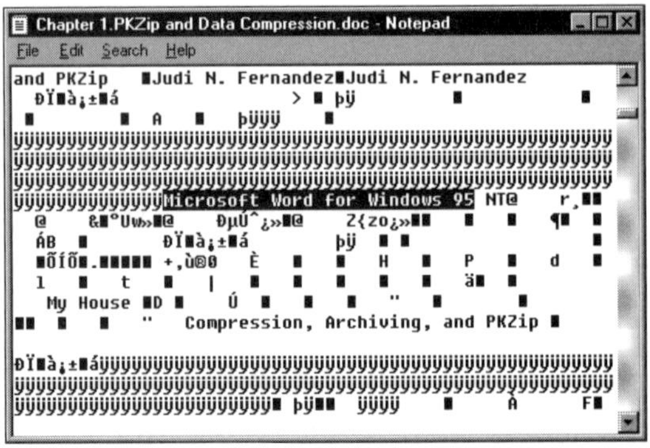

Figure 11.7 Microsoft Word's signature is farther down in the file.

Of course, some applications don't leave any recognizable signature in the document. I searched **.tar** and **.gz** files for signatures, for example, with no luck. Then you have to try some other techniques.

TRYING OUT SOME APPLICATIONS

You can often experiment with opening a document in a variety of applications just to see what happens. Many applications will recognize many formats besides their own. And with the more sophisticated applications, you don't have to tell them what kind of document it is—they can figure it out for themselves, which is exactly what you want.

I would try opening the document in your word processor, in Windows 95 WordPad if you have it, in WinZip, and in StuffIt Expander. If you have Windows 95 and have installed the Funduc Decode Shell Extension, try right-clicking the file in the Explorer to see whether you can decode it. All these products recognize several file types.

USING THE POWER OF THE INTERNET

Sometimes you have to turn to the Internet to help you identify a file type. If the file's extension is **.rem**, for example, you could search for that expression in your online service's file library, on the Web, and with search tools like Archie and Veronica. Such searches can become quite time-consuming as you wade through articles on rapid eye movement, the rock group called REM, and the DOS REM (remarks) command. But if you're desperate to interpret the file—or if you're just determined to solve the problem—the time might be worth it.

Just for fun, I searched AOL's file libraries for the expression "rem" and got back the list shown in Figure 11.8. As expected, most of the listings have to do with the rock group, but I would certainly check out the three entries called EXPANDIR, ATF, and IPRINT to see whether they offer a clue as to what a .rem file is.

File Search Results		
Category	**Subject**	**File Name**
Music Files	MOD: Do U REM Me? I REM U	IREMUREM.ZIP
Icons	ICON: 32 from FLATRich	FD_ICONS.ZIP
GIF Anime & Manga	GIF: Rem The Dream Hunter	REM.GIF
Search, Find & Chang	EXPANDIR: Expand Your Directories	EXPANDIR.ZIP
Rock Music Clips	WAV: REM: "Drive" Intro	REM.WAV
Utilities & Misc.	ATF: Thrustmaster Custom ADV	ATF2.ADV
Lyrics	LYRICS: REM: Assorted Tunes	REMWORDS.TXT
Rock Music Clips	WAV: R.E.M.: End of the World	REM.WAV
VB Utilities & Tools	IPRINT: v1.55 IntelliPrint	IPRINT.ZIP

Items 1 - 20 of 69 matching entries.

Read Description   Download Now   Download Later   Help & Information   List More Files

Figure 11.8 An AOL listing of files about "rem."

Other Internet resources, of course, are bulletin boards and newsgroups. You can post messages asking whether anyone recognizes the file type. Be sure to mention the filename, where you got the file, and any other information that might be pertinent.

TIP

Just a little note on *netiquette* (Internet etiquette). Give your request a specific subject like "Does anyone know what a REM file is?" rather than a generalized "Help!" or "I need some info." Many busy BBSers won't even read postings with vague subjects.

Online chat groups can also be helpful if you can find one on an appropriate topic. It wouldn't make much sense to drop into a group called "TV Trivia" or "Over Fifty" to ask about file types. But a group called "Computer Geeks Anonymous" or "Windows Help" might be just what you need. (These are all real names of chat groups.)

If you've never chatted online before, watch out—it's addictive. Some people find it quite threatening at first, especially if they don't type well. But they are often the ones who become the most addicted in a matter of a few days.

T I P

The Internet can also help after you've identified the file's type but don't have the software for it. Suppose that you discover the file is a photograph in Photo CD format (**.pcd**). A program like PhotoShop costs several hundred dollars. To display one image? I don't think so. But an online file search will reveal many shareware and freeware products that you can download to view and edit a Photo CD file. Choosing the best one could be a problem; you might have to download several and try them out. The folks in the photography forum can probably help you choose one, too.

A **.pcd** file is just one example, of course. No matter what type of file you're dealing with, you can probably find some shareware or freeware that can handle it. And there's probably a forum or chat group to help you choose the right software. So don't forget the power of the Internet to help you solve your problem.

Figure 11.4 is StuffIt, Figure 11.5 is a .wav file, and Figure 11.6 is GIF.

N O T E

WHAT'S NEXT?

Now that you've got the file decoded and extracted, you might have to assemble the parts before you can view or edit it. Chapter 12 shows you how to do that.

CHAPTER **12**

Splitting and Assembling Files

You saw in earlier chapters that sometimes a file needs to be split for Usenet newsgroups or for email. Even if you never split files yourself, you might sometimes need to reassemble a split file after you download all the segments. This chapter shows you how.

What you'll learn in this chapter:

- When and why files need to be split
- How to split a file
- How to download a split file
- How to assemble a file

SPLITTING HEADACHES

Neither Usenet nor Internet email can handle large files. But how large is large? There's no clear-cut answer. Different servers define their own size limits, and because you don't know what servers you're dealing with, it's pretty much a guessing game. My guess-timate is that you'll be safe with files up to 100K. If you're a belt and suspenders type, you might want to stick to 50K.

If you send a file to someone and it doesn't arrive, try again. If it doesn't arrive a second time, try splitting the file into smaller segments.

T I P

You might not need to split your own files—your mailer might do it automatically. If it encodes automatically, it probably also splits automatically. How can you tell? Send a really big file—at least couple of megabytes—to a friend on a different service without splitting it. If the person receives it, your mailer did the work of splitting.

You have to send the file to a different service. If you send it to someone on your own service, it won't have to travel the Internet and might not need to be split.

T I P

How to Split Files

Some encoding/decoding utilities will split files for you—unfortunately, WinZip will not. I don't have room on this book's disk for another encoding utility, but you can easily download one from the Internet. Of all the ones I've tried, I like WinCode from Snappy_Inc. the best. It's freeware, but you pay $5.00 to get the Help file. WinCode has an excellent interface (see Figure 12.1) and encodes, decodes, splits, and assembles files along with a few other features.

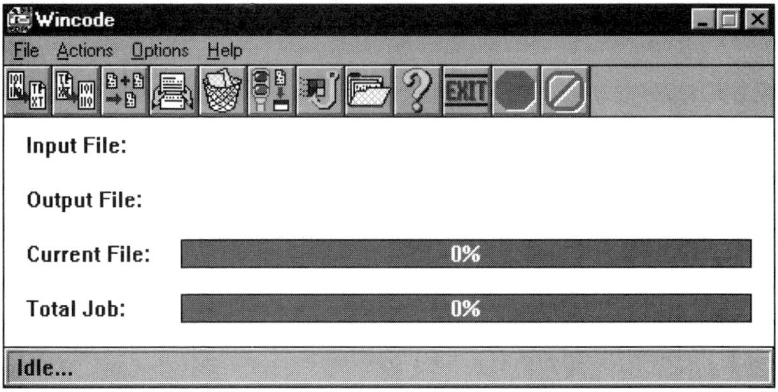

Figure 12.1 WinCode lets you split files while you encode them and assemble files while you decode them.

I prefer WinCode because it will split files as it encodes them, which I find very convenient. It also splits files between lines rather than in the middle of a line—that's not necessary, but I like it. You can find WinCode in America Online's software library (search for "WinCode") and at http://www.members.global2000.net/snappy/snappy/software.html.

Here are some other programs you might want to consider:

- Intercode 3.0 for Windows from Carrot Utilities (Shareware fee $28)

This program splits files as it uuencodes them, and you can specify the desired file size in numbers of lines so that each segment starts and ends with a whole line. But I find the nonstandard Windows interface difficult to use, especially for changing directories. Intercode also decodes and displays files. You can download it from AOL or CompuServe (search the software libraries for "Intercode") or from ftp://ftp.netcom.com/pub/ts/tsgonzo.

- Directory Toolkit from Funduc Software for Windows 95 and higher (Shareware fee $20)

  This program has a good interface, but file splitting is a separate task, and you have to specify the desired size in bytes. It's almost impossible to come up with a file size that results in whole lines for every segment. Directory Toolkit encodes, decodes, splits, and assembles files as well as filling in several gaps in Explorer's functionality (such as comparing files). You can download it from http://home.sprynet.com/sprynet/funduc.

- ZR FileWorks Omega from Scandere Software for Windows 3.x (Shareware fee $36)

  This is one of those "Swiss army knife" programs that do everything from playing CDs to encoding, decoding, splitting, and assembling files. File splitting is a separate task from encoding, and you have to specify the file size in bytes. The interface is unusual but not hard to figure out. You can download it from many online services and BBSs, as well as many Internet sites, such as ftp://winsite.com/pub/pc/desktop/zrfw801.zip.

- Omega from Scandere Software for Windows 95 (Shareware fee $36)

  This is the Windows 95 version of ZR FileWorks Omega.

If you don't have any software to do it for you, you can split encoded files manually using any good ASCII text editor. You can also use your word processor if it can save a file in ASCII text format—and most of them can. The exact steps you follow depend on whether your editor/word processor can open two documents at once. I prefer Microsoft Word over WordPad for this task because it's much easier to work with multiple documents. I'll show two procedures here: the first is for editors that can open multiple documents, and the second for editors that can open only one document at a time. In both cases, you must uuencode the file before splitting it.

How to split a file using multiple documents:

1. Open the encoded file in your editor.
2. Select about 1,000 lines (60,000 bytes) and press **Ctrl+Insert** to copy them to your Windows Clipboard.

Don't drive yourself crazy trying to count 1,000 lines. I hold down **Shift** and press **PageDown** about 45 times. (I can count to 45.) That selects about 1,000 lines.

T I P

3. Choose **File|New** or click the **New** icon to open a new file.
4. Press **Shift+Insert** to paste the lines from the Clipboard.
5. Choose **File|Save** to save the new file.
6. Name the new file *name*1.uue.

Be sure to save the file as an ASCII text file. It won't get through the Internet if you save it in your word processor's native format.

T I P

7. Close the new file and return to the original file.

   The lines should still be selected.

8. Click at the beginning of the *next* line.

   This deselects the previous set of lines and positions the cursor so that you can select the next set.

9. Repeat steps 2 through 8 to create *name2*.uue, *name3*.uue, and so on until you finish segmenting the original file.

The final segment might be a lot shorter than the others. That's okay.

T I P

How to split a file using only one file at a time:

1. Open the encoded file in your editor.

2. Select about 1,000 lines (60,000 bytes) and press **Ctrl+Insert** to copy them to your Windows Clipboard.

3. Click at the beginning of the *next* line to put the typing cursor there.

4. Insert an easy phrase to remember at the beginning of the line, (see the circled text in the following example):

NOTE

Inserting an easy-to-find phrase will help you find where you left off when you reopen the file.

5. Choose **File|Save** to save the file under its original name.

6. Choose **File|New** or click the **New** icon to open a new file.

7. Press **Shift+Insert** to paste the lines from the Clipboard.

8. Choose **File|Save** to save the new file.

9. Name the new file *name*1.uue.

TIP

Be sure to save the file as an ASCII text file. It won't get through the Internet if you save it in your word processor's native format.

10. Close the new file.

11. Open the original file.

12. Search for the phrase you inserted in step 4.

13. Delete the inserted phrase.

14. Repeat steps 2 through 13 to create *name2*.uue, *name3*.uue, and so on, until you finish segmenting the original file.

The final segment might be a lot shorter than the others. That's okay.

T I P

When you finish, how do you know that you split the file successfully? The best way is to reassemble it (explained later), decode the result, and make sure that you still have a valid file. If not, try again.

EMAILING OR POSTING SPLIT FILES

When you email split files or post them on Usenet, be sure to mark their sequence numbers like this:

Whitehouse photo (1/4)

Whitehouse photo (2/4)

Whitehouse photo (3/4)

Whitehouse photo (4/4)

The expression (1/4) tells others that this is part one of a four-part file. They know to look for the other three parts, which might not be next in the list.

ASSEMBLING SPLIT FILES

In the sample mail list in Figure 12.2, a friend sent me a six-part file. I received it as six different letters, which I had to download individually. Then it was up to me to assemble the parts into a complete file. I had to assemble them *before* I decoded them, or the decoder wouldn't be able to produce the right result.

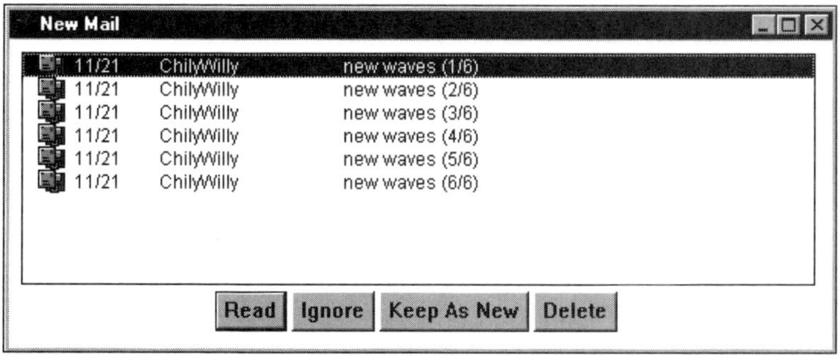

New Mail			
11/21	ChilyWilly	new waves (1/6)	
11/21	ChilyWilly	new waves (2/6)	
11/21	ChilyWilly	new waves (3/6)	
11/21	ChilyWilly	new waves (4/6)	
11/21	ChilyWilly	new waves (5/6)	
11/21	ChilyWilly	new waves (6/6)	

Read Ignore Keep As New Delete

Figure 12.2 A split file list looks like this in my email list.

Let's look at another example, this one from Usenet. Figure 12.3 shows what a split file looks like on a Usenet newsgroup. In this case, all parts of the file appear in sequence, so your job is easy. Sometimes the parts are separated, and you have to go looking for some of them.

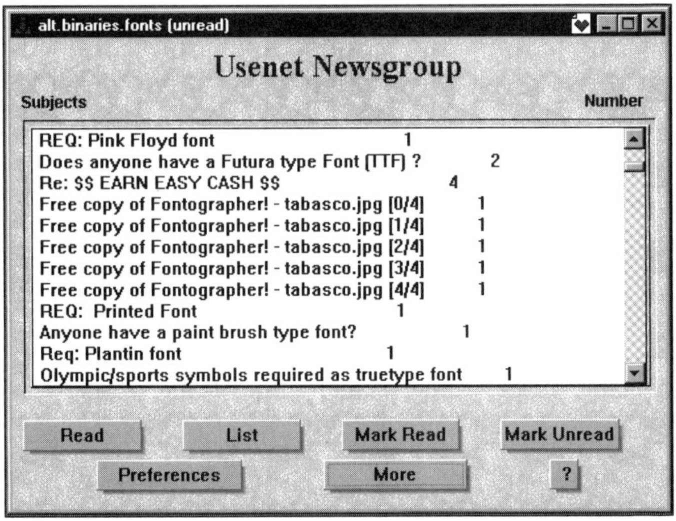

Figure 12.3 Here's a split file on Usenet.

Several of the programs I mentioned earlier can be used to assemble split files: WinCode, Directory Toolkit, ZR FileWorks Omega, and Omega. If you don't have a program to assemble your files, you can do it manually. It's not nearly as hard as splitting them because you don't have to keep track of where you left off. Just keep in mind that you're trying to create a valid uue file: it starts with the *begin* line, then has so-many lines of encoded data one after the other with no interruption, then a blank line (which might contain an apostrophe), and finally the *end* line. (The last data line might be shorter than the others and might not start with M.) There can be comments before the *begin* line and after the *end* line, but not in between.

How to assemble split files:

1. Open the *second* file in an ASCII text editor.

That's right. You start with the second file. You're going to copy it into the first file.

T I P

2. Select all the text and press **Ctrl+Insert** to copy it to the Windows Clipboard.

3. Close the file and open the *first* file in the series.

4. Press **Ctrl+End** to position the typing cursor at the end of the file.

5. If the last line is complete, press **Enter** to start a new line.

If it's not complete, you need to piece the line together, so don't press **Enter**. Let the next insert start at the end of the current line.

N O T E

6. Press **Shift+Insert** to paste from the Clipboard.

7. Choose **File|Save** to save the new data in the file.

8. Open the next file in the series.

9. Repeat steps 2 through 8 until all the files have been copied into the first file in the proper sequence.

If your editor has an **Insert|File** command, the process is much easier:

1. Open the first file in your editor.

2. Press **Ctrl+End** to position the cursor at the end of the file.

3. Choose **Insert|File**.

    A browse box appears.

4. Select the next file in the series and click **OK**.

5. Repeat steps 2 through 4 until all the files have been inserted.

6. Choose **File|Save As** to save your newly assembled file. Be sure to save it as an ASCII text file.

If you don't mind using a complicated DOS command, there's an even faster way to assemble files. It uses the concatenation feature of DOS's COPY command. Here's how:

1. Open an MS-DOS command prompt window.

2. Use the CD command to change to the directory containing the segmented files. If the files are in your **\internet\download** directory, for example, you would enter **cd \internet\download**.

3. Enter a command like the one shown below, but replace *target.uue* with the name of the file you want to create, and *segment1.uue*, *segment2.uue*, *segment3.uue*, and so on with the names of the segmented files. You're not limited to three segmented files as shown in the example. You can add together as many files as you can fit on the 127-character command line.

```
copy segment1.uue+segment2.uue+segment3.uue target.uue
```

Now let's assume that you have assembled the file by one of the preceding methods. At this point, your new file may or may not be ready to decode. Some programs, and some people too, insert comments into file segments. Figure 12.4 shows an example of three file segments that were encoded and split by

ZR FileWorks. The first two lines of each file are comments inserted by the encoder:

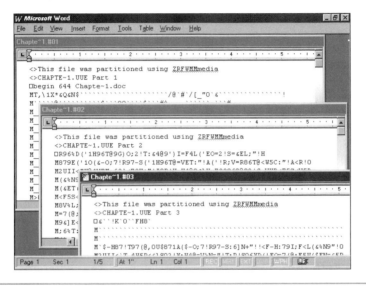

Figure 12.4 ZR FileWorks inserted comments when it split this file.

You could leave the comments at the beginning of the first file—your decoder ignores any text before the word *begin*. And you can ignore any comments after the word *end* in the last file. But all other comments must be removed. The lines of encoded data must follow each other without any interruption. When the file is assembled correctly, you shouldn't be able to tell where it was split.

What's Next?

You're probably more than a little concerned that downloading files from the Internet makes your system vulnerable to computer viruses. The next section explains viruses (and other nasties) and shows you how to protect your computer.

PART IV

Computer Viruses

CHAPTER 13

An Introduction to Computer Viruses

Does this sound like you? "I don't really need to worry about computer viruses. After all, I don't know anyone who has ever caught one. And I don't do anything to endanger my system." If so, your computer could be living on borrowed time.

Computer viruses are very real and are proliferating at an alarming rate—about 1,000 new viruses a year right now, and that number is growing. I have caught a couple of viruses, as have several of my friends. And if you ever download files or swap diskettes with friends, you can too.

What you'll learn in this chapter:

- What viruses are (and what they aren't)
- Other types of programs that are related to viruses: trojan horses, worms, and ANSI bombs
- What a mail bomb is (and isn't)
- How you catch viruses (and how you don't catch them)
- How to fight viruses with scanners and activity monitors

MY OWN EXPERIENCES WITH VIRUSES

I have encountered a couple of viruses in the past few years. In one incident, a coauthor emailed me some Microsoft Word documents that were infected with not one, but two viruses. The viruses quickly spread to many of my other Word documents. Fortunately, they were harmless viruses, two of the first Word document viruses, and relatively easy to get rid of after I discovered them (see Figure 13.1).

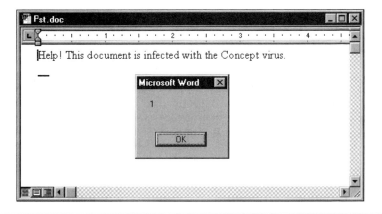

Figure 13.1 *My system incurred the WM.Concept virus, which displays a "1" when you open an infected document.*

NOTE   They say that the first Microsoft Word viruses, including WM.Concept, were created by a virus researcher trying to demonstrate to his colleagues that such a virus was possible. Unfortunately, the viruses got away from the researchers and are now "in the wild"—meaning that they have spread to the point where they can't be contained.

In another incident a few years ago, I rented a computer that came complete with the Stoned virus—no extra charge. Fortunately, I scanned it before loading my software on it. I'm usually an easygoing person, but I sure gave that rental company a piece of my mind for sending out an infected computer.

Here's a frightening story that happened to me just yesterday. I was doing research for this chapter, looking up the latest information on viruses on the Internet, just to be sure that I hadn't missed anything new and significant. I called up my favorite Web crawler and searched for "virus." The first references that came back were for a page named simply "Virus" that promised much information on viruses.

Well, good! That's what I wanted! So linked to the page. But it turned out to explain how to write viruses—oops, not what I wanted after all. I backed up and followed some more fruitful links. About 15 minutes later, my Web browser began acting up. I closed it down and restarted it, but it was still acting funny. Hmmmm. About that time I remembered that page I had visited. I wondered...could it have done something to my browser?

So I decided I had better do a virus scan. And guess what— my antivirus software was gone. It had disappeared from my Start menu, and its folder was empty except for one file called **uninstal.exe,** with a date of last week (see Figure 13.2). (I had last updated my virus scanner a month ago, so this program did not belong there.) Eee-yikes! I did *not* run that uninstall program. I quickly downloaded an up-to-the-minute scanner and scanned for viruses. The result: no viruses found. But I'm taking some extra precautions for the next few months.

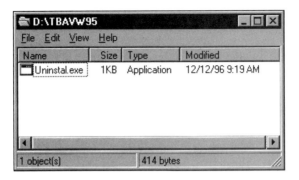

Figure 13.2 *This lone file replaced my antivirus software after I visited a Web page about viruses.*

WHAT IS A VIRUS?

It's difficult to come up with a succinct definition of the term *virus* that everyone would accept. But most experts would agree that a virus has these characteristics:

- It is *executable*. It might be a program, a macro, a Java applet, or something similar, but whatever it is, it's capable of performing functions on your computer.

- It *replicates* itself. It can copy itself from one place to another (from a floppy disk to your hard disk, for example). Viruses spread by replication, much like cancer.

- It *invades* your system. You don't intentionally install it; it sneaks in uninvited. How? It might be hidden in a program or document that you download, or it might replicate itself from a floppy disk to your hard disk.

- It attempts to *hide* in your system. It might insert itself into your other programs, into your boot sector (explained shortly), or in a document.

- It may lie *dormant* for a long time. It doesn't deliver its payload (the trick that it plays or the damage that it does) until it has had plenty of time, perhaps months, to spread itself throughout your system and infect other systems from yours. By the time you discover it, you no longer can trace back to where it came from.

SUPPOSEDLY HARMLESS VIRUSES

Not all viruses have damaging payloads (see Figure 13.3). Some are meant as jokes—they might play a little tune or display a funny message. Many are simply someone's way of saying, "Gotcha!" They might simply display a message or perhaps not do anything at all.

Figure 13.3 *The JoJo virus displays this kaleidoscopic screen; but because of bugs, it can hang up your system or worse.*

The problem with "harmless" viruses is twofold. First, they inspire others to try their hands at writing not-so-harmless viruses. Second, most viruses operate at a very low level, meaning that they bypass your operating system. Such programs require extra knowledge and experience to write correctly, along with rigorous testing and debugging. But most viruses are written by young teens with a minimum of knowledge and experience and no patience for testing. Many of these viruses are full of bugs that can harm your system in ways their authors never intended. So even the "cute" and "harmless" viruses need to be rigorously avoided.

N O T E I probably created a pre-virus in the 1950s when I sneaked some code into a friend's program that printed "Help! I'm being held prisoner in an IBM 650!" every so often in his printouts. I was 16 years old, and I thought it was hilariously funny. My code didn't replicate or hide itself, though, so I can't claim to have created the first virus. Darn.

THE NASTY VIRUSES

The most famous viruses, of course, are the malicious ones—the ones that wipe out your hard drive or delete all your **.doc** files, often on a particular date such as the programmer's birthday. These are the ones that attract a lot of media attention and for good reason—they do as much worldwide property damage as a hurricane or earthquake. Fortunately, their own fame makes them relatively easy to stop because antivirus software soon appears to detect and remove them.

VIRUS HOAXES

A couple of the most famous viruses are merely hoaxes. If you're online much, you'll eventually receive a warning about the Good Times virus. I receive a nearly hysterical letter every few months describing the horrible things it will do to my computer. The rumor must be endlessly circling the Internet, like the Nieman-Marcus cookie recipe (another myth that arrives in my mailbox every few months). It's not real; there is no Good Times virus. Nor is there an Irina virus, a recent hoax launched by a publisher trying to promote a new book (not MIS:Press).

T I P The Good Times hoax claims to be a virus that attacks and destroys your system as soon as you open an email with the subject "Good Times." Now why would someone who wants to spread a virus make it so easy to spot? Don't worry about this one, there's no way to get a virus simply by opening an email—yet.

Just because a few virus rumors are groundless doesn't mean you can afford to ignore every warning that comes your way. It pays to check out each rumor before deciding whether it is real or bogus. (See "Some Handy Internet Sites" at the end of this chapter for some good places to check.) The most recent rumor to land in my mailbox was about the Hare virus, which is a very real virus and a very nasty piece of work. I didn't have it as it turns out, but I'm still glad that I paid attention to the rumor and downloaded some software especially to detect and counteract the virus.

N O T E As I edit this, another warning has arrived in my mailbox. This one concerns the Deeyenda virus, which will attack and destroy my entire system as soon as I open an email with the subject "Deeyenda." Sound familiar? The Deeyenda virus is also a hoax.

DOCUMENT MACRO VIRUSES

It used to be that a virus had to reside in an executable file, such as a **.bat, .exe,** or **.com** file. No document could contain a virus because documents aren't programs. But in today's word processors and other applications with programmable macro features, document viruses are now possible. More than possible, they are a reality. As I write this, there are nearly a dozen known Microsoft Word macros that can infect documents on Microsoft Word 6.0 or higher (the first version of Word that had programmable macros). There are also a few Excel and AmiPro document viruses.

Most of these viruses are jokes and gotchas. But as always, one person's joke becomes another one's statement and the next one's spite. Just recently, we're seeing the first destructive Word macro viruses, ones that delete the current document or all the documents in the current directory.

A Word macro virus arrives in a document and inserts itself into **normal.dot,** the base template used by every Word document. It might take the form of an *auto macro*—that is, a macro that is executed automatically when you start word, open or close a document, or exit Word. Or they might replace some of the commands on your menus, such as **File|Save** or **Tools|Spelling.** Either way, a macro virus is fairly easy to get rid of, after you realize that you have it. You'll see how in the next chapter.

Boot Record Viruses

The first sector on every disk contains a small program called a *boot record* that is executed when you boot from that disk. Even if the disk is not bootable, it must have a boot record. On a nonbootable floppy, for example, the boot record simply displays a message such as "Nonsystem disk or disk error. Replace and press any key." On a bootable disk, the boot record loads the operating system so that you can use your computer.

Hard disks have multiple boot records. The primary one—the one on the first sector—is called the *master boot record* or *MBR*. You'll sometimes hear boot record viruses referred to as MBR viruses.

NOTE

Boot record viruses are the most popular. About 70 percent of known viruses are boot record viruses. Why? Because the boot record gets loaded first, before the operating and your antivirus software. A boot record virus has time to hide itself or deliver its payload before you can do anything about it. When you suspect that you have a boot record virus, you have to boot from a clean floppy—that is, one that you *know* is free of viruses—and then clean up the infected boot record. More about that in Chapter 14.

Do you have a clean, bootable floppy? You should. I'll show you how to make one in Chapter 14.

TIP

VIRUS COUSINS

There are several other kinds of antisocial programs out there that technically aren't viruses, but most people include them when they use the word *virus*. I can't think of any antivirus software that limits itself to viruses and doesn't also look for trojan horses and worms, for example. Throughout this book, except in the preceding section where I defined the term, when I say *virus* I really mean all these kinds of antisocial programs.

WORMS AND TROJAN HORSES

If a program promises something that's hard to believe, don't believe it—it's probably a worm or a trojan horse. "Just download and install this program, and you'll get to use America Online FREE OF CHARGE—and it's perfectly legal!" No thanks. "WE'LL PAY YOU $1,000 to try out our new software!" Yeah, right.

A *worm* is a freestanding program that replicates itself and delivers some kind of payload—malicious or otherwise. The difference between a worm and a virus is that the virus is a parasite that invades other programs. The worm has its own program file. Remember the story I told you at the beginning of this chapter about my antivirus software disappearing? That **uninstal.exe** program on my hard drive was probably a worm.

A *trojan horse* is a freestanding program, usually harmful, that does not replicate itself. It spreads because it promises something people want. Programs available on the Net purporting to be release 2.5 (or higher) of PKZip are trojan horses, for example.

Some trojan horses are hacker programs that appear benign. They might even do something fun or useful. But they secretly search your hard drive for information about you— your account passwords; your real name, address, and phone number; your credit card numbers; and so on. The next time you sign on, they email the information back to their programmers, who attempt to use the information to run up huge bills on your accounts.

ANSI Bombs

Your system might load a driver called **ANSI.SYS** that lets DOS applications redefine your keyboard, among other things. **ANSI.SYS** used to be very popular in DOS, and it was required by many DOS-only programs, but it is not used in Windows. Unfortunately, many systems still load the **ANSI.SYS** driver because no one has ever told it to stop. Not only does this take up unnecessary memory space, it also makes you vulnerable to ANSI bombs when you're using the DOS command prompt screen (ANSI bombs can't function in Windows).

TIP

How do you stop loading **ANSI.SYS**? Edit your **c:\config.sys** file and put REM in front of the line that says something like this:

`DEVICE=C:\ANSI.SYS`

Then reboot your system. If you find that some of your DOS programs no longer work and you still want to use them, remove the REM and reboot again. Then be extra careful to avoid ANSI bombs.

An ANSI bomb may or may not be a program. It could be just a document file containing **ANSI.SYS** commands that redefine your keyboard. If it's a joke, it simply moves all your keys around so that when you try to type *Now is the time*, it comes out *Str xp vlk vxqk*. A more malicious bomb assigns destructive DOS commands to your keys—as you keep pressing various keys trying to figure out what happened to your keyboard, you destroy your system.

Rebooting may clear your keyboard (if your system is still there). But if the bomb has inserted itself into your **AUTOEXEC.BAT** file, it will redefine your keyboard again during booting. You'll need to boot from a clean diskette and delete the ANSI bomb.

A NOTE ABOUT MAIL BOMBS

Many people have heard the frightening term *mail bombs* and believe them to be some kind of virus that activates when you open and read a letter. That's not possible. Letters aren't software, and nothing in a letter (so far) can hurt your system.

A mail bomb consists of hundreds or thousands of copies of the same letter (see Figure 13.4). You can imagine how irritating that would be, and how hard it would be to find your legitimate mail mixed in with the bomb fodder. But mail bombs are not destructive, just annoying.

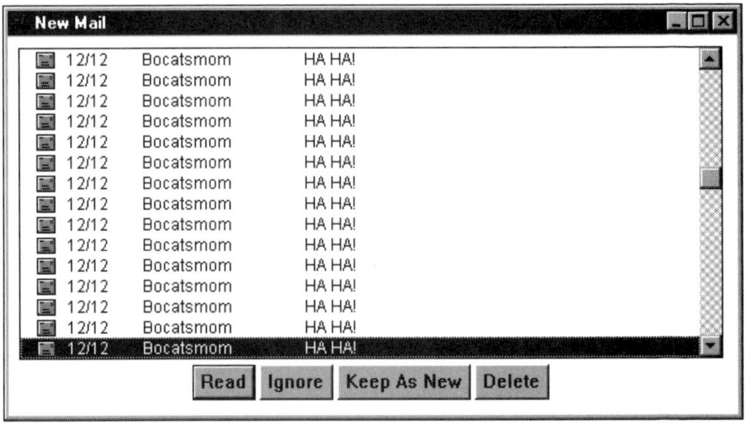

Figure 13.4 *Oh noooo! I've been mail bombed!*

CATCHING VIRUSES

How do you catch a virus? Any time you expose your computer to the outside world, you might be exposing it to a virus. So if you sign on to a network, a local BBS, or the Internet, your chances of catching a virus increase. Similarly, if you insert a removable disk, tape, or cartridge into your computer, the risk goes up. But some activities are riskier than others, and some online activities involve no risk at all.

The most common source of boot record viruses is infected media such as CDs, diskettes, tapes, and various types of cartridges. If the media is new and has not yet been formatted, the risk is very low, although it's still there and you should scan it before using it. Somewhat riskier are preformatted media and software disks in their original shrink-wrapped packages. Even though software providers take every precaution to make sure that their products are virus-free, sometimes a disgruntled employee manages to sneak one through.

NOTE I have heard of a couple of viruses, including one of the Word macro viruses, appearing on disks shipped by Microsoft. I have also heard stories of government agencies shipping viruses on disks going out to potential bidders on research projects.

The risk increases when the media comes from a less professional source. Friends sharing diskettes probably accounts for the most widespread boot record viruses. If a buddy gives you a disk for any reason, regardless of whether it contains software, scan that disk. Remember that *all* disks contain software in the boot record. If you accidentally boot from an infected floppy, the virus is activated and can invade your system.

Networks, bulletin boards, and the Internet are prime vehicles for transmitting viruses. You can get them by downloading files from email and Web, FTP, newsgroup, BBS, and forum sites— any site where you can download a file.

Can you get a virus just by visiting a Web site, as apparently happened to me? Maybe yes, maybe no. Many Web browsers respond to Java applets, programs that are triggered when you enter the page or click a certain function. Java applets jazz up Web pages with animation, sound, and interaction, as shown in Figure 13.5; they are definitely the wave of the future. Because Java applets are programs, theoretically they could contain viruses, but none has been reported so far. But I swear that something wiped out my antivirus software yesterday.

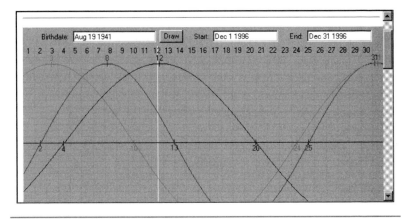

Figure 13.5 A Java applet makes this Web page interactive.

Some online activities are perfectly safe. You can't get a virus from chatting, reading and writing email (but see the tip that follows), or reading newsgroups and other noninteractive sites unless you download files from them.

Virus experts warn of the possibility that full function mailers that automatically download attached files might download an infected file. If the mailer goes on to attempt to load the file, the virus could be activated.

T I P

THE WAR AGAINST VIRUSES

Enter the guys in the white hats—the antivirus researchers. They spend their time investigating the latest viruses and figuring out how to identify and remove them from people's systems. For many of them, it's more than an occupation, it's a crusade.

IDENTIFYING NEW VIRUSES

When a new virus is reported, the researchers examine the program and determine what it does. They give it a name based on some characteristic they find in it, such as Stoned or Michelangelo. Then they try to figure out some way to detect and remove it from people's systems. Let's look at the ways viruses can be detected.

Scanning for Virus Signatures

One way of detecting a virus is to look for a *signature*—a unique string of code that can be used to spot the virus in your system. For example, suppose that the Greetings virus, shown in figure 13.6, displays the message, "Greetings from Judi Fernandez! You must type 'Hi Judi' to continue." (I made this virus up for the purpose of this example. There is no known Greetings virus.) A researcher might decide that this virus's signature is "Greetings from Judi Fernandez!"

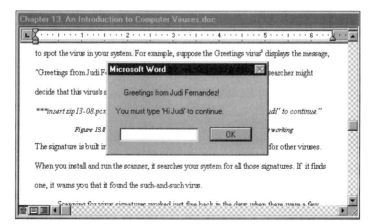

Figure 13.6 *My hypothetical virus forces you to type "Hi Judi" to continue working.*

The signature is built into a virus scanner along with thousands of signatures for other viruses. When you install and run the scanner, it searches your system for all those signatures. If it finds one, it warns you that it found the such-and-such virus.

Scanning for virus signatures worked just fine back in the days when there were a few hundred viruses and only one or two new ones a month. Nowadays, this methodology is becoming increasingly cumbersome. Here's why:

- With more than 6,000 viruses to scan for, virus scanners have become huge programs, requiring a lot of space in memory and on your hard disk. It takes so long for them to do a full scan, comparing everything on your system to every virus signature, that you might be tempted to scan less often. Even worse, you might hesitate to download the latest version of a scanner because the download time is so long. For this reason, researchers are starting to take shortcuts, such as looking for shorter signatures, looking for signatures that can be used for multiple viruses, and scanning only parts of your system. Such shortcuts can lead to other problems.

- An ill-chosen signature can yield *false positives*—identifying viruses where there are none. For example, suppose that a scanner tries to use the shorter "Fernandez!" rather than the full phrase "Greetings from Judi Fernandez!" as a signature. It might find on your hard disk a Web page titled "Viva Fernandez!" and a letter in which you say, "I finally finished that book by Fernandez!" Many people panic when their virus scanner tells them they have a virus, so false positives can cause much anguish. Not only that, but if a major scanner, used by hundreds of thousands, identifies a false positive in a popular program such as PKZip or Lotus 1-2-3, the rumor spreads that the software is infected, and its reputation is damaged. This has happened a few times and has led to lawsuits.

- Another source of false positives is having two or more signature scanners on your hard disk. Because a scanner must have its virus signatures built into its program files, those signatures are stored on your hard disk where another virus scanner can find them. Every scanner knows not to identify itself as a virus, but if you have a second scanner in your system, scanner A might not recognize scanner B and might report it as an infected file. Every antivirus company develops its own signatures, so scanner A and scanner B probably look for different signatures. But if they have just one signature in common—which is not too unbelievable considering how many viruses and signatures there are—then each could spot the other one as an infected file. To circumvent this problem, most of the leading scanners encode their signatures for storage and decode them only during scanning. However, not all scanners do this, so false positives can occur with some scanners.

TIP   This is not to say that you shouldn't have two or more signature scanners. In fact, I think you should have at least two if you want maximum protection, as discussed in the next chapter. But you need to apply some common sense when scanner A identifies scanner B as infected.

- As soon as a new scanner is released, the virus programmers analyze it for its signatures and release variations, called *virus strains*, that don't use those signatures (see Figure 13.7). For example, the Greetings virus might be adapted to say "Greetings from Judi N.

Fernandez!" or "Hello from Judi Fernandez!" It only takes a few minutes to create a new strain because only a few lines have to be changed. Unfortunately, it takes much longer for the strains to get back to the antivirus researchers and updated scanners circulated. And of course, with each new signature, the virus scanner gets a little longer, and we've already discussed the problems that causes. (The problem of keeping up with the latest viruses and strains has become so oppressive and expensive that some of the early antivirus leaders have dropped out of the field.)

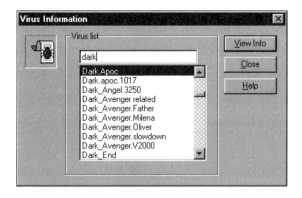

Figure 13.7 *Some strains of the Dark Avenger virus (listed by McAfee's VirusScan for Windows).*

- Most computer users don't update their scanners often enough. They might keep a scanner for a couple of years (or until a new virus scare makes the front pages). So new viruses and new strains spread much faster than new signatures. This can lead to *false negatives*, where a scanner reports no viruses in your system, giving you a false sense of safety, when in fact there is a virus.

Despite these problems, scanners are the most popular antivirus tools, so researchers are trying to find other ways to scan for viruses.

Heuristic Scanning

A newer scanning technique is to look for virus-like code rather than specific signatures. For example, a scanner might look for any code that tries to insert something into the boot record, any code that reformats a hard drive, and any code that deletes all *.doc files. This *heuristic scanning* is much more efficient. It's also more effective against viruses that have not yet been identified. But it can also lead to false positives because some programs legitimately perform these tasks. And, of course, some virus programmers know exactly what heuristic scanners look for and try to create code that won't be spotted.

Integrity Checking

The viruses that spread the fastest and do the most damage are the new ones—the ones that have not yet been identified and signatured. Heuristic scanners provide one line of defense against unidentified viruses. Another method involves identifying changes to software files. Most program files do not change after they have been installed. Any change is therefore suspect. If your **msword.exe** file suddenly gains 200 more bytes, for example, you must be very suspicious that it has been invaded by a virus.

An *integrity checker* keeps track of statistical data about your program files, such as their sizes and date/time stamps. Each time you scan your hard drive, it compares the current statistics against its recorded statistics. Any disparities are reported as possible viruses (see Figure 13.8). Because it's fairly easy for a virus to invade a file without changing its size or date/time stamp, an integrity checker also calculates a numeric value, much like the CRC value discussed in chapter 8, for each program file. If a virus overwrites 200 bytes in a file, the size won't change, but the CRC will.

Virus Detected !

Virus Information
D:\COLLAGE\collage.exe has been changed!

Heuristic flags:

C The checksum data does not match! File has been changed!
p Packed program. A virus could be hidden inside the program.

Action to take
- Clean file
- Delete file
- Kill file
- Rename file
- Validate
- Continue
- Non-stop continue
- Quit

Ok
Virus Info
Help

Figure 13.8 This file failed the integrity check, but that doesn't mean it has a virus.

An integrity checker on its own can't identify specific viruses. Nor can it clean (remove) a virus from an infected file. It merely tells you that a program file has changed somehow and might be infected. So integrity checkers usually work in conjunction with other types of scanners to provide complete antivirus coverage.

TIP

If you find that every directory on your hard drive contains a file with a name like **Checklst.ms** or **antivir.dat** and you have no idea how they got there, don't erase them. They contain your integrity checker's statistics.

Integrity checking can also lead to false positives. If you upgrade a program, for example, your integrity checker will report the upgraded files as possibly infected. It's up to you to remember that the change is intentional and can be ignored.

The biggest problem with relying solely on integrity checking is the assumption that new software is virus-free. When you install a new program, your integrity checker has no previous statistics to compare it to. On the first scan after installing the program, the integrity checker finds the new files and calculates and records their statistics. If the program is already infected, the integrity checker will not identify the infection.

NOTE   Some programs now include their own antivirus mechanism so that, when you install them and every time you run them, they can check their own integrity. And some software takes advantage of PKZip's Authenticity Verification feature, discussed in Chapter 8, to guarantee that you receive the program files virus free.

Another obvious problem with integrity checking is that it cannot protect document files. You would hardly want your scanner to warn you every time you change a word processor or spreadsheet document. So integrity checking is limited to program files only.

Although integrity checking on its own does not provide sufficient protection against viruses, it is one important factor in a complete antivirus plan. When you're choosing your antivirus software, make sure that it does integrity checking along with signature and/or heuristic scanning. Most of the leading scanners include an integrity checking component.

ACTIVITY MONITORS

Most virus programmers aren't clever or skilled enough to create viruses that can evade detection by scanners and integrity checkers. But a few viruses can, so you might need another level of protection. An *activity monitor* is a memory-resident program that detects and blocks virus-like behavior in your system. You start it up when you boot, and it stays in the background, monitoring everything that goes on.

As a minimum, an activity monitor prevents programs from doing highly suspect things such as writing in an executable file, writing in a boot record, or reformatting a hard disk. With many monitors, you can opt for more protection, up to the level of intercepting every disk write until you authorize it, scanning every program and document that you load, and scanning all removable media before you can use them.

Used in conjunction with up-to-date scanners, activity monitors can dramatically increase the effectiveness of your antivirus plan, but you can probably see why they're not as popular a scanners. Even at their lowest level of protection, they consume valuable system resources and impede your overall system performance. At maximum levels, they can bring your system to its knees. I can't imagine anyone—not even a security freak—living with that level of protection for very long.

Getting Rid of Viruses

Detecting a virus is only half the problem. Getting rid of it is the other half. In the case of trojan horses and worms, all you have to do is delete the offending file. Macro viruses are also easily removed by deleting the macros. But what about true viruses, the ones that invade a program or the boot record? You don't want to completely delete the host or replace the boot sector unless you have to. Here are some alternatives:

- Your antivirus software can probably *clean* a known virus—that is, it can delete the viral code from the infected file or boot record. If it can't completely extract the virus, it might be able to remove enough to disable the virus. Most of the time, the cleaned file is still usable, although in some cases the virus may have damaged the host file.

- For unknown viruses in files that you can't afford to delete, you can disable the virus by changing the file's extension to something that is not executable and then try to get the virus identified so that it can be cleaned.

- You could replace the infected file with a clean version. For a program file, you might need to reinstall the program if you can't replace just the infected file from the original disk. For document files, you should be able to restore the file from its backup if your backups are up-to-date and virus-free.

When your antivirus program detects or suspects a virus, it tells you what your options are. They usually include cleaning the virus (if possible), deleting the file, or not taking any action. You choose the last option when you want to handle the virus yourself or when you know that no virus is present. We'll talk more about these options in the next chapter.

THE NEW COLD WAR?

For every new defense technique, there's a virus programmer somewhere trying to overcome it. So we're involved in an ever-escalating war: better viruses, better antiviruses, still better viruses, still better antiviruses, ad naseum. No one can predict where it will all end, but at the moment it looks like the viruses will win out in the long run, in part because the virus programmers work for fun, whereas it's becoming forbiddingly expensive and time-consuming to counteract them.

RECENT VIRUS ADVANCES

The past couple of years have seen some dramatic increases in virus techniques, such as *polymorphic viruses*, which constantly change themselves to avoid having signatures. Even more disturbing, *virus generators* are now easily available— programs that make it simple for a beginner to create and release a virus. (Remember that Web page I stumbled into at the beginning of this chapter?) Fortunately, the generators are not very good at this time, and the viruses they produce are buggy and easy to detect. But you have to assume tomorrow's generators will be more effective.

ADVANCED ANTIVIRUS TECHNIQUES

The antivirus techniques discussed so far—various types of scanners and monitors—suffice for most home users and many small businesses. Larger organizations, where it is impossible to control what employees are going to stick into a floppy drive or copy to a network drive, probably need some advanced defenses. And, of course, the more important the data, the more it needs to be protected regardless of the size of the organization. We hopefully can assume that the White House, the FED, the SEC, the Pentagon, and the Social Security Administration are doing more than an occasional virus scan. Can we make the same assumption about our insurance carriers, creditors, doctors, banks, and the like? I hope so; but I'll tell you the truth, my fingers are crossed as I write this.

I'm assuming in this book that you are not responsible for protecting a system at an advanced level. If so, you need more help than I can give you here. So I'm just going to overview the types of techniques used in high-risk systems:

- Hardware defenses such as write-protected hard drives and nonbootable floppy drives.

T I P You might be able to set up your computer to boot first from the hard drive rather than drive A. This helps to prevent accidental boots from floppy disks that might be infected. Check your hardware documentation to see whether you can do this on your computer.

- *Diskette fences*—systems that permit only their own removable media; media created or updated by another system cannot be accessed.
- Utilities that let you write-protect your software.
- Antivirus protection built into the master boot record or BIOS to prevent virus activity during booting.

WHAT'S NEXT?

Are you thoroughly depressed now? I am—just from doing the research and writing this chapter, even though I knew and have written about it before. But chin up; the next chapter shows you how to protect your system from the dark side of the Internet.

CHAPTER 14

Scanning for Viruses

I hope the preceding chapter scared you a little. Not too much—there's no need to panic—but just enough to convince you to scan every executable file as soon as you download it. Do you also need to scan files before you prepare them for uploading? Not if you're confident that your system is virus-free because you follow a rigorous antivirus plan. But if you're not absolutely sure, do your friends a favor and scan every file before you send it.

Because this book is about handling Internet files, I have to limit this chapter to the subject of scanning incoming and outgoing files. It would take several chapters to talk about a complete antivirus strategy: deciding what to do when, how to scan all or part of your system, how to set up a monitor, how to tell when you have a virus, and so on. If you need additional help with these topics, look for a good book on virus protection.

What you'll learn in this chapter:

- How to avoid viruses on the Internet
- Where to find three popular scanners: Dr. Solomon's FindVirus, McAfee VirusScan, ThunderByte TBAV
- How to make a clean boot disk

- How to scan your entire system with these three scanners
- How to scan selected files with these scanners
- What to do if your scanner reports a known virus
- What to do if your scanner reports an unknown virus

A FEW SIMPLE RULES FOR AVOIDING VIRUSES ON THE INTERNET

You can't completely avoid viruses on the Internet, but you can significantly reduce your risk of exposure by applying a little common sense:

- Download files only from reliable sites.
- Choose moderated boards.
- Download attached files only if you know who sent them to you.
- Inspect all self-extracting files before extracting them.

DOWNLOAD FILES ONLY FROM RELIABLE SITES

You're much less likely to download a virus from Microsoft's Web site than from Honest John's Weekly Software Picks. When you want to download some new software, look for a "name brand" site. But always be aware that this does not completely protect you from viruses. Microsoft and other reputable dealers have inadvertently spread a few viruses. But the key word here is "inadvertently." They don't do it on purpose; they try to prevent it. Less reputable sites might not be so considerate.

CHOOSE MODERATED BOARDS

When a bulletin board, newsgroup, or software library is unmonitored, anyone can upload anything to it, and the risk of infected files goes sky high. But when a board is moderated, someone inspects messages and files before they are posted.

Most moderators reject messages and files that aren't appropriate to the topic of the board. Do they also scan files for viruses? Many do, but some don't. Even when they do, they might not be using the latest or the best scanner, so you can't assume that a moderated board is completely safe. But the probability of downloading a virus from it is a lot lower than from an open board.

How can you tell if a board is moderated? There might be a message saying so, or there might be a separate folder for submitting messages and uploading files. Look for a way to post to a board yourself. If you can post something on the board easily, so can everyone else. If you have to send your post to a special place or if you can't post at all, the board is much more restricted.

It's often easier to tell if a board is not moderated because pyramid operators post "get rich quick" messages to almost every board they can get their hands on. Figure 14.1 shows a typical example from a board that is supposed to be about Atari. But this board has more messages about making money than about Atari. This is clearly not a moderated board.

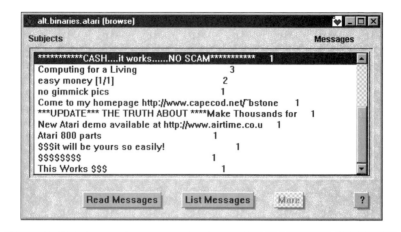

Figure 14.1 *Those "get rich quick" messages tell you that this board is not moderated.*

Download Attached Files Only If You Know Who Sent Them to You

Never download a file from a stranger, especially if the accompanying letter makes unbelievable promises. Even your friends aren't safe because they might pass viruses along without realizing it. But only fools download files from strangers.

Inspect All Self-Extracting Files Before Extracting Them

Anyone can claim that a **.exe** file is a self-extracting file. When you run it to extract it, you could be running a trojan horse instead. Listing the contents of the file in PKZip or WinZip tells you immediately whether it's a self-extracting file. You'll get an error message like the one in Figure 14.2 if the file is a program rather than a self-extracting archive.

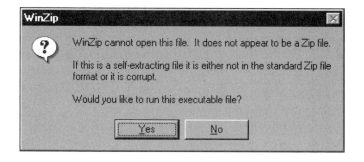

Figure 14.2 *This WinZip message tells you that a file is not a valid archive—be sure to click* **No**.

WHICH FILES ARE SUSPECT?

The preceding chapter talked about the types of files that are suspect: executable files and any file that can contain a programmable macro. Let's look specifically at what files you need to scan:

- Executable files—look for these extensions:

386	com	exe	sys
bat	drv	fon	vxd
bin	dll	ovl	

- Any document or template files for Microsoft Office 6.0 or higher applications, regardless of the their extensions
- Any document files for AmiPro regardless of their extensions
- Any document files for any of your applications that permit programmable macros, regardless of their extensions

If your system loads **ANSI.SYS,** you also need to check any files that you'll be using under DOS rather than Windows. **ANSI.SYS** commands can be buried in text documents as well as programs. Most scanners do not check text documents for ANSI bombs, although WinZip does.

YOUR ANTIVIRUS SOFTWARE

Why didn't I include some antivirus software with this book? I'm afraid if I give you a program you'll think, "Well that's good enough—I'll just use that for the next year or two." Instead, you should learn where the Web sites are and download updates regularly—at least once a month and whenever a new virus is making the rounds. No scanner is 100 percent effective, so you should have several of them. That way, if one scanner reports a virus, you can check it with your others. Or if you suspect a virus but your first scanner doesn't find it, you can look for it with the others.

THREE POPULAR SCANNERS

This section briefly describes three popular and highly rated scanners. Two of the them, ThunderByte and McAfee, are shareware and can be downloaded from the Internet. You can try them out before paying for them. You can also download Dr. Solomon's FindVirus for evaluation purposes, but you have to pay in advance if you want Dr. Solomon's entire antivirus package. All three of these scanners, however, make updates available on the Internet so that you can easily keep these products up to date.

Dr. Solomon's AntiVirus Toolkit

Dr. Solomon's AntiVirus Toolkit includes several components:

- **FindVirus,** a signature and heuristic scanner and cleaner (see Figure 14.3)
- **Scheduler,** which sets up an automated schedule for FindVirus
- **WinGuard,** a VxD that automatically scans files as you download, copy, and access them in Windows

NOTE   VxD is a *virtual device driver,* the Windows equivalent of a memory-resident program, but a VxD consumes much fewer system resources.

- **VirusGuard,** the DOS version of WinGuard, which also intercepts **Ctrl+Atl+Del** and prevents you from accidentally rebooting from an infected floppy
- **ViVerify,** an integrity checker

Figure 14.3 *You can download FindVirus for DOS to try out before buying the package.*

You can try out FindVirus for DOS but not the other components. You can download it from these sites:

CompuServe: GO DRSOLOMON

America Online: keyword VIRUS

Prodigy: FILE LIBRARIES (Antivirus Center)

FTP: ftp.drsolomon.com/pub/findvirus

Web: http://www.drsolomon.com

Dr. Solomon's BBS : (617) 229-8804 v.34, N81

McAfee VirusScan

McAfee (pronounced MACK-a-fee) antivirus products include these components:

- **VirusScan,** a signature scanner and integrity checker for Windows (see Figure 14.4)
- **VShield,** a VxD activity monitor
- **WebScan,** which automatically scans executable, **.zip,** and Microsoft Word files that you download via email or your Web browser
- **Scan for DOS,** which you use when a virus is detected or suspected and you want to boot from a clean copy and scan without starting up Windows

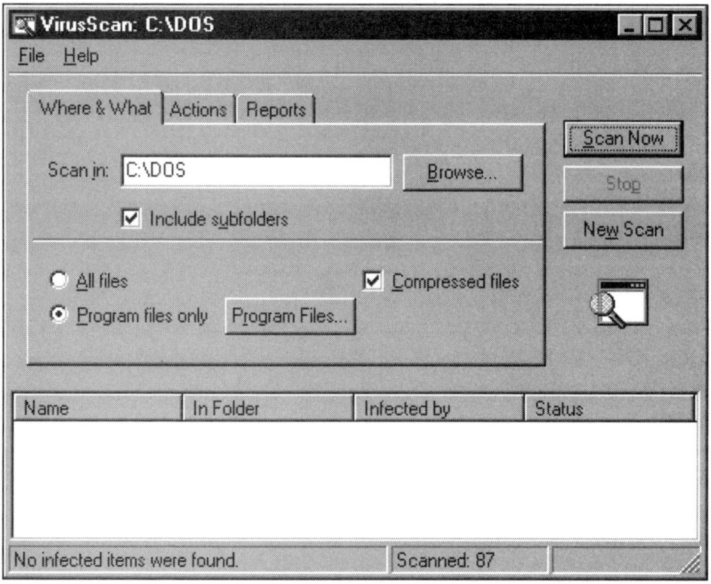

Figure 14.4 You can evaluate McAfee shareware for 30 days.

The McAfee antivirus products are distributed in a shareware version and a retail version. I prefer the shareware version because it is more likely to be up to the minute; the retail version could be a few months old when you buy it from a dealer's shelf. You can evaluate the shareware version for 30 days. If you decide to keep it, the shareware fee is $65. You'll find it at these sites:

America Online: keyword MCAFEE

CompuServe: GO MCAFEE

Microsoft Network: GO MCAFEE

Web: http://www.mcafee.com

FTP: ftp.mcafee.com

ThunderByte TBAV

TBAV is a signature scanner, heuristic scanner, and integrity checker (see Figure 14.5). It includes an optional background scanning feature that periodically scans your system as you work. It also includes a VxD that automatically checks the files that you access and the diskettes that you insert in a floppy drive.

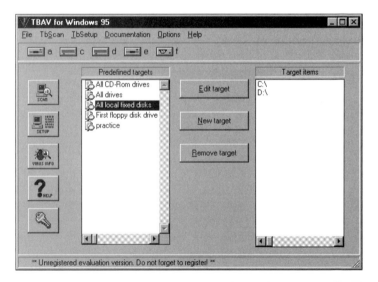

Figure 14.5 *You can download TBAV from the ThunderByte sites.*

TBAV for Windows does not remove viruses because the ThunderByte folks believe that you should always clean viruses under DOS, not Windows. All experts agree that you should boot from a clean floppy before you remove a virus. ThunderByte recommends that you then avoid loading Windows and do the removal in DOS. Hence, only TBAV for DOS includes a cleaning component.

You can download ThunderByte TBAV from these sites:

America Online: keyword VIRUS

CompuServe: GO TBYTE

FTP: ftp.thunderbyte.com

Web: http://www.thunderbyte.com/

MAKING A CLEAN BOOT DISK

When your antivirus software detects or suspects a virus, the first thing you should do is boot from a clean (uninfected) floppy disk. This gets the virus out of memory, so that it can't replicate itself or deliver its payload. Then rerun your scanner.

If you don't have a clean bootable floppy disk, make one right now. Your system needs to be free of viruses to do this. If you know or suspect that your system is already infected, it's too late to make one on your system. But you might be able to make one on a friend's system, if your friend has the same version of Windows that you have.

SCANNING YOUR ENTIRE SYSTEM

Before you start making the disk, check your system for viruses. The following procedures show you how to do that for each of the three scanners. They assume that you have already downloaded and installed the necessary software.

NOTE If your scanner reports a known or unknown virus at any point while you are trying to make a bootable floppy, stop the process, shut down your system, and make your bootable floppy somewhere else. Then follow the procedures under Dealing With Known Viruses later in this chapter.

How to check your entire system using Dr. Solomon's FindVirus:

1. The evaluation version of FindVirus runs in DOS, so open a DOS prompt window.

    a. If you're using Windows 95 or higher, choose **Start|Programs|MS-DOS Prompt**.

    b. If you're using Windows 3.*x*, open the **Main** group and then double-click **MS-DOS Prompt**.

2. Switch to the drive and directory where you stored the Dr. Solomon program files. For example, if they are in **c:\findv**, you would enter this command:

```
cd \findv
```

3. Enter the following command, which tells FindVirus to scan all your drives using heuristic analysis:

```
findviru /alldrives /analyze
```

It will take a while for FindVirus to complete the task, so sit back and relax. FindVirus first checks the integrity of its own **.exe** file. Then it scans memory. And then it scans all your drives. Your screen will appear as follows while it scans the drives:

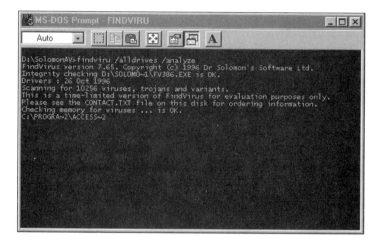

4. When the job finishes, FindVirus displays a summary of the results. Read the messages to make sure that no viruses were found.

5. Press any key to end the job.

You can enter the following command to see the complete command syntax for the findviru command:

T I P   `findviru /help`

How to check your entire system using McAfee VirusScan:

1. Start up VirusScan.

   After displaying a splash screen (the program's logo), VirusScan scans memory. Then you'll see the following window:

2. Click the **Browse** button and select one of your drives.

3. Click the **Scan Now** button.

   During the scan, the window expands to show a status line and a list of all the infected files, as shown below:

4. Repeat steps 2 and 3 until all your drives have been scanned.

How to scan your entire system using ThunderByte TBAV:

1. Start up ThunderByte.

   You'll see a splash screen (the program's logo) while ThunderByte scans memory. Then you'll see the window shown below:

2. In the Predefined Targets list, select **All Drives**.

3. Click the **Scan** button.

   ThunderByte displays a progress window as shown below:

```
TbScan                                                              ×

   [icon]    The Thunderbyte Anti-Virus utilities provide a collection of sophisticated
             programs which offer various ways to check for, identify and remove known as
             well as unknown viruses from hard and floppy disks on PCs or across
             networks.

C:\PROGRAM FILES\COMMON FILES\MICROSOFT SHARED\NOTE-IT\

   MSINFO32.EXE      Win95/NT   w           Ok    Signatures:        3997
   MSQRY32.EXE       Win95/NT   w           Ok    Directories:         44
   ORGCHART.EXE      Win95/NT   w           Ok    Total files:        467
   ARTGALRY.EXE      Win95/NT   w           Ok    Executables:        120
   EQNEDT32.EXE      Win95/NT   w           Ok    CRC verified:         0
   MSDRAW.EXE        Win95/NT   w           Ok    Infected items:       0
   WRDART32.EXE      Win95/NT   w           Ok    Changed items:        0
 > NOTE-IT.EXE       Win 16-bit w           Ok    Elapsed time:   0:00:10
                                                  KB / second:       1329

                          [    Stop    ]
```

MAKING THE BOOTABLE DISKETTE

Now that you know your system is clean, you're ready to make
the bootable diskette. The correct procedure depends on the
version of Windows that you're using. Both procedures follow.

How to make a bootable floppy with Windows 3.*x*:

1. Insert a new diskette in drive A.

Be sure to use drive A. You can't boot from any other disk drive.

T I P

2. Open the **Main** program group.
3. Start **File Manager.**

4. Choose **Disk|Format Disk** to open the dialog box shown below.

5. Enable **Make System Disk,** so that there is an X in the box.

6. Click **OK.**

   A message box warns you that all data on the diskette will be destroyed and asks whether you're sure.

7. If you're sure, click **Yes.**

   It takes a minute or so to format the disk. Then a message box asks whether you want to make another disk.

8. Click **No.**

9. When the disk is ready, try booting with it to make sure that it works.

10. Reboot from your hard drive.

How to make a bootable floppy with Windows 95 and higher:

1. Insert a new diskette in drive A.

    Be sure to use drive A. You can't boot from any other disk drive.

T I P

2. Choose **Start|Settings|Control Panel** to open the Control Panel.

3. Open **Add/Remove Programs** to display the window shown below:

4. Click the **Startup Disk** tab.

5. Click **Create Disk**.

6. When the disk is ready, try booting with it to make sure that it works.

7. Reboot from your hard drive.

When the diskette is ready, label it clearly and store it where you can find it six months from now. (I keep one of mine tacked to the bulletin board above my desk and a second one with my backup disks.)

SCANNING SELECTED FILES

All three scanners discussed in this chapter can scan selected files. You can use them to scan files that you have just downloaded or files that you are about to upload. The following procedures show you how.

How to scan selected files with Dr. Solomon's FindVirus:

1. Start up a DOS window if necessary.
2. Switch to the drive and directory containing the FindVirus program files.
3. Enter a command using the following syntax:

```
findviru pathname
```

or

```
findviru /checklist=pathname
```

With the DOS version of Dr. Solomon's FindVirus—which is the only downloadable version—you include the necessary pathnames in the command that you use to start the scanner. It's easy when you need just one pathname, which can be a single filename, a generic name, or the name of a directory. For example, all the following are legitimate commands:

```
findviru \projects\t21\report1.doc
findviru \programs\*.exe
findviru \internet\download\
```

When multiple pathnames are involved, the easiest way to handle them is to place the list of pathnames in a separate file and reference that file in the findviru command. But only single pathnames can be used in a file list. For example, suppose that **filelist.txt** contains this list:

```
\projects\t21\report1.doc
\programs\caution.exe
\programs\practive.com
\programs\prmaker.dll
\internet\download\lookup.exe
```

The following command would cause all the preceding files to be scanned:

```
findviru /checklist=filelist.txt
```

The other two scanners are easier to use because they have Windows interfaces. With McAfee, you can open the VirusScan window and select an entire directory to scan (you can't select individual files from the VirusScan window). Or, if you chose the necessary option when you installed VirusScan, you can right-click files in Explorer and select a scan option from the context menu.

How to scan a selected directory from the VirusScan window:

1. Start up VirusScan.

   After displaying a splash screen (the program's logo), VirusScan scans memory. Then you'll see the main VirusScan window.

2. Click the **Browse** button and select the desired directory.

3. Click the **Scan Now** button.

How to scan selected files from an Explorer window:

1. Select the files that you want to scan.

TIP

You can do this from any Explorer-type window, including My Computer, Find, and similar windows.

2. Right-click any of the selected files to pop up the context menu.

3. Choose the **Scan** option from the context menu.

How to scan selected files with ThunderByte TBAV:

1. Start up ThunderByte.

    You'll see a splash screen (the program's logo) while ThunderByte scans memory. Then you'll see the main TBAV window.

2. Click the **New Target** button to open the window shown below:

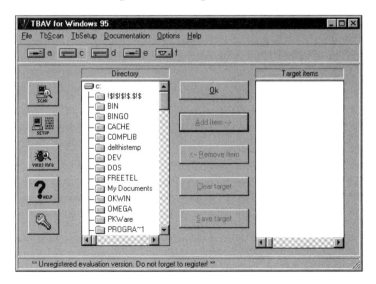

3. In the drive list (below the menu bar), click the drive containing the files you want to scan.

    The drive's directories appear in the **Directory** list.

4. In the **Directory** list, open one directory containing the files you want to scan.

5. In the **Directory** list, select the desired files.

6. Click **Add Item** —> to add the selected files to the **Target Items** list.

You can add an entire directory to the Target Items list by selecting the directory without opening it and then clicking the **Add Item** —> button.

T I P

7. Repeat steps 4 through 6 until all the desired files on this drive appear in the **Target Items** list.

8. If more than one drive is involved, repeat steps 3 through 7 until you have selected all the desired files.

9. If you would like to save this list of files for future use, click the **Save Target** button and give the list a name.

10. Click the **Scan** button to scan the items listed in the **Target Items** list.

DEALING WITH KNOWN VIRUSES

Suppose that you get a message like the one shown in Figure 14.6. In the example, ThunderByte has found a known virus, the Concept virus, in a Microsoft Word document. (I have been saving this virus for a long time so that I have a real example to show when I write lessons on viruses.) What would you do now?

Virus Detected !   ⊠

┌─Virus Information─────────────────────────────────┐
   D:\MSOFFICE\TEMPLATES\PUBLICATIONS\PPGSTYLE.DOC
         infected by WordMacro/Concept {1} virus

   Heuristic flags:

┌─Action to take─────────────────────────────┐   ┌────┐
   ○ Clean file   ○ Validate   │ Ok │
   ○ Delete file   ○ Continue   └────┘
   ○ Kill file   ○ Non-stop continue   │ Virus Info │
   ⊙ Rename file   ○ Quit
                                              │ Help │

Figure 14.6 *My scanner has reported a virus and is waiting for*
me to decide what to do.

The first thing to do is really a don't: Don't panic. Some people freak out when their antivirus software reports a virus. But you can't make rational decisions in a state of panic, so stay calm and proceed methodically. Remember, it could be a false positive.

Next, discontinue the scan immediately. In the example in Figure 14.6, I would click **Quit** in the **Action to Take** section and then click **OK**. This terminates the scan in ThunderByte.

Next, close down all programs and shut down your computer. Then restart using your clean boot floppy disk. This is known as a *cold boot.*

Don't just reboot with **Ctrl+Alt+Del**, which is known as a *warm boot*. Many viruses are smart enough to intercept **Ctrl+Alt+Del** and keep themselves going even though you think you've rebooted.

T I P

Now, run a different scanner. Does it find the same virus? If not, try some more scanners, including the original one, but do a cold boot before each scan. (If you don't do a cold boot each time, a scanner might pick up the trace of the previous scanner's signatures in memory and mistakenly identify them as one or more viruses.) If no scanner finds the virus a second time, the original report might have been a false positive. Or you might have cleaned the virus out of memory when you rebooted. Or you could be dealing with a mutating virus. So the next step is to download the latest versions of your virus scanners and try again. If you still don't find a virus, you'll have to give up, but you should probably take a few steps for safety's sake:

- If the virus was reported in a file, delete the file in question or replace it from its backup (which you should also scan).
- Install and use an activity monitor for the next few months.
- Scan much more often.

If your scanners do locate the virus a second time, you have to decide how to handle it. If cleaning is an option, you might want to consider it. However, be aware that removing a virus from a file doesn't always restore the file to a usable condition. If you just downloaded the file, contact the sender and ask for a clean file. If that's not feasible and you really need to keep the file, then you'll have to try cleaning it.

Figure 14.7 shows how McAfee VirusScan reports the same virus. To clean the document, you would click the **Clean** button.

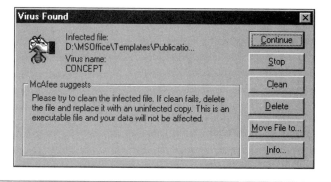

Figure 14.7 Another look at the same virus.

By the way, notice the **Info** button in Figure 14.7 and the **Virus Info** button in Figure 14.6. You can click these buttons to see much more detailed descriptions of the virus in question.

DEALING WITH UNKNOWN VIRUSES

Your scanner might report a suspected unknown virus rather than a known one. Figure 14.8 shows a typical example, where ThunderByte's integrity checker has discovered that a program file has been changed.

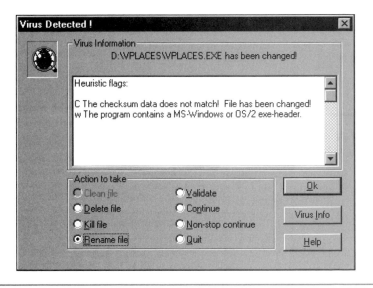

Figure 14.8 My integrity checker reports that a program file has changed.

Here again, rule number one is, don't panic. In this case, a moment's clear thought helps me remember that I just downloaded an upgrade to the program, so naturally the program file has changed. It's nice to know that my integrity checker is working just fine. In this case, I select **Validate** to tell ThunderByte to update its records with the new version of the program. Then I click **OK** to continue.

But not all unknown viruses are so easily solved. Figure 14.9 shows a case where a program has triggered a few red flags in the heuristic analyzer. If I wasn't a programmer, I wouldn't have much of an idea what the messages mean, but there's enough there to know that this file might contain an unknown virus. Now what?

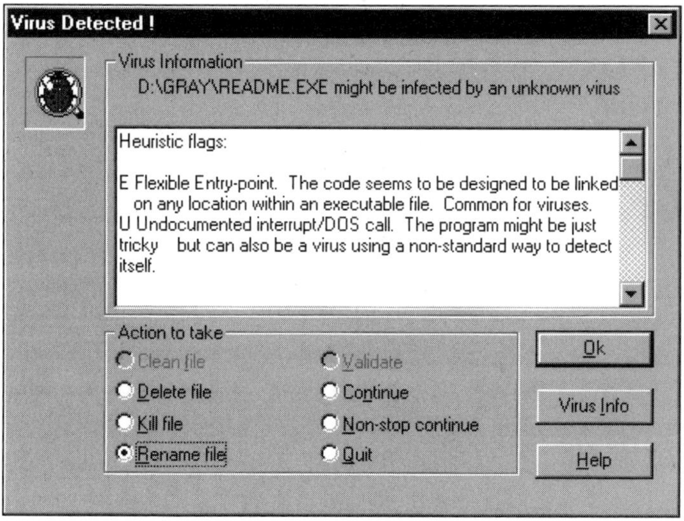

Figure 14.9 A heuristic analyzer.

The first thing you would do is rename the file—get rid of that .exe extension so that it's no longer executable. Then terminate the scan and do a cold boot. Your next step would be to try to turn the unknown virus into a known one by checking the file with all your scanners. If none of them recognize the virus, bring them all up to date and try again.

If you still can't identify a known virus and you don't want to just kill the file, it's time to seek outside help. Each of your scanners should have a way of reporting unknown viruses. Check the documentation that comes with the scanner to find out how to do it. A virus research center can usually turn a new unknown virus into a known one very quickly so that within a few days you'll probably be able to identify and clean the virus.

Don't forget to let the people who sent you the virus know what happened. They will need to deal with the virus on their systems too.

T I P

WHAT'S NEXT?

You have completed all the chapters in the book! I hope by now you're feeling much more comfortable with files from the Internet and email. The last part of this book comprises step-by-step procedures for downloading and uploading, zipping and unzipping, and encoding and decoding using a variety of programs and services. Good luck ... and enjoy!

PART V

Checklists

It's so hard to remember all the steps necessary for uploading and downloading files on the Internet. This part gives you some checklist procedures that you can follow for America Online, CompuServe, Microsoft Network, Netscape, and Eudora Light. (AT&T WorldNet uses Netscape and the mail handler of your choice.) Some of these procedures are repeated from earlier chapters, but many appear only in this part. I'm including an extra table of contents to help you find the procedures that you need.

Contents of Part V

AMERICA ONLINE

Based on America Online version 3.0 for Windows (WAOL 3.0).

NOTE

TO ATTACH A FILE TO EMAIL

1. Zip the file or files, if desired.

America Online's mailer includes MIME, so you don't need to encode files.

TIP

2. Click the **Compose Mail** icon to open a blank letter, as shown below.

3. Fill out the address and subject and write a note to accompany the file.

AOL won't send a letter when the body is blank.

NOTE

4. Click the **Attach** icon.

   AOL opens a browse dialog box where you can locate and select the file to be attached.

5. Select the file and click **Open**.

   AOL attaches the file to the letter, as shown below.

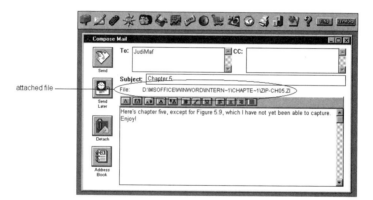

6. Click **Send** to send the file.

To Download a File from Email

1. Open the letter to which the file is attached.

2. Click the **Download Now** button.

   A progress dialog box keeps you informed while the file downloads.

3. Sign off, if desired. You don't need to be online for the remaining steps.

4. Decode the file, if necessary.

5. If the file was zipped and AOL didn't unzip it automatically when you exited, unzip the file now.

6. If any executable files were added to your system, scan them for viruses.

TO DOWNLOAD A FILE FROM AOL SOFTWARE LIBRARIES

1. Locate the desired file in a software library, as shown below:

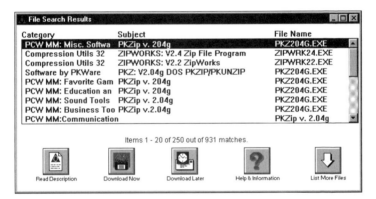

2. Select the file and click **Download Now.**

A progress dialog box keeps you informed while the file downloads.

3. Sign off, if desired. You don't need to be online for the remaining steps.

4. Decode the file, if necessary.

5. If the file was zipped and AOL didn't unzip it automatically when you exited, unzip the file now.

6. If any executable files were added to your system, scan them for viruses.

To Download a File from FTP

1. Go to keyword FTP to open the FTP dialog box shown below:

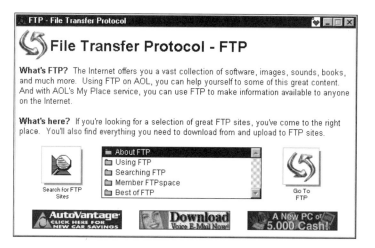

2. Locate the FTP site that you want to download from.

3. Select the file you want to download.

4. Click the **Download Now** button to open a common Windows Save As dialog box.

5. Select the desired directory for the file and click **Save**.

    A progress dialog box keeps you informed while the file downloads.

6. Sign off, if desired. You don't need to be online for the remaining steps.

7. Decode the file, if necessary.

8. If the file was zipped and AOL didn't unzip it automatically when you exited, unzip the file now.

9. If any executable files were added to your system, scan them for viruses.

To UPLOAD A FILE TO FTP

1. Go to keyword **FTP** to open the FTP window.

2. Locate the FTP site that you want to upload to.

3. Click the **Upload** button.

   A dialog box asks for the name and type of the file.

T I P

If the **Upload** button is not available, the site cannot receive uploaded files.

4. Type the name of the file as it should appear on the FTP site and click **Continue**.

T I P

The name you type here is not necessarily the name of the file on your hard disk. It is the name by which the file will be stored at the FTP site.

An Upload File dialog box appears, as shown below:

```
┌─────────────────────────────────────────────┐
│ ▫ Upload File                    _ □ ☒       │
│ ┌────┐                                       │
│ │ ▣  │                                       │
│ │    │                                       │
│ └────┘                                       │
│  Send                                        │
│ ┌────┐                                       │
│ │ ◈  │                                       │
│ │    │                                       │
│ └────┘                                       │
│ Select                                       │
│  File                                        │
│ File:                                        │
│ ┌─────────────────────────────────────────┐ │
│ │                                         │ │
│ └─────────────────────────────────────────┘ │
└─────────────────────────────────────────────┘
```

5. Click **Select File** to open a common Windows browse dialog.

6. Select the file to be uploaded and click **Open** to return to the Upload File dialog box.

7. Click **Send** to upload the file.

    A progress box keeps you informed while the file is uploading.

To download a file from the Web

1. Open the Web site that contains the file you want to download.

2. Click the link to the file to open a common Save As dialog box.

3. Select a directory and click **Save**.

    The download progress is displayed in the status bar (the bottom line) of the browser window.

4. Sign off, if desired. You don't need to be online for steps 4, 5, and 6.

5. Unzip the file, if necessary.

6. If any executable files were added to your system, scan them for viruses.

To download a file from a newsgroup

1. Go to keyword **USENET**.
2. Locate the desired newsgroup.
3. Select a file you want to download.
4. Click **Download Now**.
5. If the file is encoded, AOL asks if you want to download the original file—that is, if you want AOL to grab all parts of it and decode it—or download just the current "article." The message is shown below.

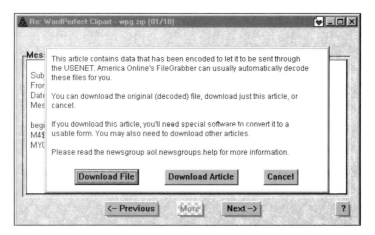

6. Click **Download File**.
7. Sign off, if desired. You don't need to be online for the remaining steps.
8. Unzip the file, if necessary.

9. If any executable files were added to your system, scan them for viruses.

To Upload a File to a Newsgroup

1. If the file is binary, uuencode it, splitting it into several small files, if necessary.

2. Sign on and go to keyword **USENET**.

3. Locate the desired newsgroup.

4. Click **File|Open** to open a standard Windows browse box.

5. Select the file you want to upload.

   AOL displays the file in a generic editing box.

6. Press **Ctrl+A** to select all the text in the file.

7. Press **Ctrl+Insert** to copy the text to the Windows Clipboard.

8. Go back to the newsgroup window and click **Send New Message**.

9. Click the body of the message to put the typing cursor there.

10. Press **Shift+Insert** to paste the encoded file into the window.

11. Give the message a subject.

Don't forget to add a sequence number, such as (1/3), if this is a multipart file.

T I P

12. Click **Send**.

13. Repeat steps 4 through 12 to send all the segments of a split file.

COMPUSERVE

Based on CompuServe 3.0.1 for Windows.

NOTE

TO ATTACH A FILE TO EMAIL

You can do all of the following offline.

TIP

1. Scan the file for viruses, if necessary.
2. If it's a binary file and you're sending it to someone outside of CompuServe, encode the file.

CompuServe does not automatically encode binary files.

TIP

3. From the main menu, click the **Mail Center** button to bring up the Mail Center screen.
4. Click **Create** to open the Create screen.
5. Click **New** to open the Create Mail window, as shown below:

6. Address and write the letter as desired.

7. Click **Attach File** to open a common Windows Open dialog box.

8. Locate and open the file you want to attach. An **Attach Files** dialog box appears, as shown below:

9. If you're sending the file outside of CompuServe (via the Internet), make sure that **File Type** says **Text**. If not, follow these steps:

  a. Click the file to select it. (Very important, even if there's only one file in the list.)

  b. Drop down the **File Type** list and select **Text**.

10. If you want to attach more files, click **Add to List**.

11. Repeat steps 8 through 10 until all desired files are attached to the letter.

12. Click **OK** to close the dialog box and return to the Create Mail dialog box.

The **Attach File** button shows the number of files attached, as in **Attach File: 1**.

13. If you decide later that you want to attach more files, click **Attach File** to reopen the Attach Files dialog box. Then repeat steps 10 through 12.

14. Send or file the message as desired.

To DOWNLOAD A FILE FROM EMAIL

You can do all of the following offline except step 3.

1. From the main menu, click the **Mail Center** button to bring up the Mail Center screen.

2. If it's not already selected, click **Read** to bring up the Incoming Messages screen, as shown below:

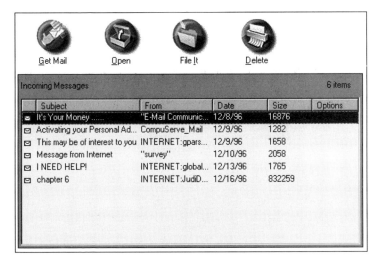

3. If you have not yet retrieved your mail from CompuServe, click the **Get Mail** button. CompuServe will sign you on and retrieve your mail.

You might want to sign off again before going on to step 4.

T I P

4. Select the message you want to read and click **Open** to open it, as shown below:

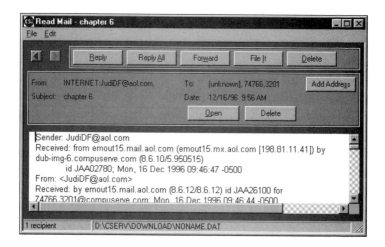

5. Click **File It** to save the file on your hard disk.

6. Decode the file, if necessary.

7. Unzip the file, if necessary.

8. Scan the file for viruses, if it's an executable file.

If you extracted several executable files from a zipped archive, be sure to scan them all.

T I P

TO DOWNLOAD A FILE FROM FTP

1. Click **Go** to open the Go screen.

2. Type **ftp** or select **FTP** from the list of **Services Recently Visited**.

   A message warns you about some of the inherent dangers of FTP.

3. Click **Proceed** to continue to the ftp screen, shown below:

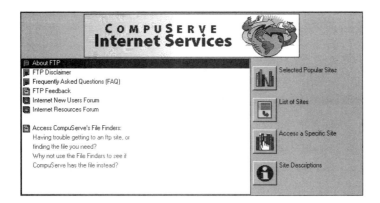

4. Locate the site containing the file you want to download. As an example, one of my sites is shown below:

Current Site: users.aol.com			
Current Files: /judinorth/*.*			
Directories	Files		Size
.	☐ propert1.jpg		67634
..	☐ propert3.jpg		73483
private	☐ propert4.jpg		72188
	☐ propert5.jpg		150603
	☐ propert6.jpg		99799
	☒ redhorse.ani		18722
	☐ sysinfo.jpg		98276
	☐ sysinfo1.jpg		146965
	☐ sysinfo2.jpg		58685
	☐ sysinfo4.jpg		1455
	☐ sysinfo5.jpg		1626
	☐ th-judi.gif		7725

Select Top Back Leave   View   Retrieve   Upload   Filter

5. Click the checkboxes next to the files you want to download so that each box contains an X.

6. Click **Retrieve**.

    A common Windows Save As dialog box appears so that you can designate where you want to save the file.

7. Select the desired directory and click **Save**.

A progress dialog box keeps you informed while the file downloads.

8. Sign off, if desired. You don't need to be online for the remaining steps.

9. Decode the file, if necessary.

10. Unzip the file, if necessary.

11. If any executable files were added to your system, scan them for viruses.

TO UPLOAD A FILE TO FTP

1. Click **Go** to open the Go screen.

2. Type **ftp** or select **CIS: ftp** from the list of **Services Recently Visited**.

A message warns you about some of the inherent dangers of FTP.

3. Click **Proceed** to continue to the FTP screen.

4. Locate the site you want to upload to.

The site you select must permit uploads.

T I P

5. Click **Upload**.

A message box warns you that you must have the rights to any file that you upload.

6. Click **OK** to proceed.

An Upload dialog box lets you select the file you want to upload, as shown below:

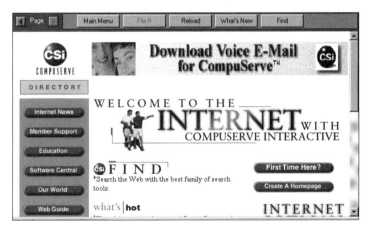

7. Type the pathname of the file or click **File** and select the file.

8. Select the correct **File Type**.

9. Click **OK** to upload the file.

To download a file from the Web

1. Click **Go** to open the Go screen.

2. Type **web** or select your Web site from the list of **Services Recently Visited** to open the Web browser shown below:

3. Locate the site containing the file you want to download.

You can go directly to a site by entering the URL on the Go screen.

T I P

4. Click whatever icon the site provides to download the file.

   A dialog box indicates that the file is downloading. Then another dialog box asks what you want to do with the file, as shown below:

5. Select **Save it to disk** and click **OK**.

   A common Windows Save As dialog box appears so that you can designate where you want to save the file.

6. Select the desired directory and click **Save**.

   A progress dialog box keeps you informed while the file downloads.

7. Sign off, if desired. You don't need to be online for the remaining steps.

8. Decode the file, if necessary.

9. Unzip the file, if necessary.

10. If any executable files were added to your system, scan them for viruses.

To download a file from a newsgroup

1. Sign on and go **usenet.**
2. Locate the desired newsgroup.
3. Locate the desired file.
4. Click the checkbox next to the file so that an **X** appears in the box.

Repeat steps 3 and 4 for all parts of a segmented file.

T I P

5. Select **Decoded.**
6. Click **Retrieve.**

   A standard Windows Save As dialog box appears.
7. Select a directory for the file and click **OK.**

   A progress box appears while the file downloads.

You might want to sign off to finish the task.

T I P

8. Combine the segments of the file if it was split.
9. Unzip the file, if necessary.
10. Scan any executable files that you downloaded.

To upload a file to a newsgroup

1. If the file is binary, uuencode it, splitting it into several small files if necessary.

2. Sign on and go **usenet**.

3. Locate the desired newsgroup.

4. Click **Create** to open a Create Usenet Message dialog box.

5. Click **Upload** to open an Upload dialog box.

6. Click **File** to open a common Windows Open dialog box.

7. Locate and select the file.

8. Make sure that the **File Type** says **Binary**.

9. Click **OK** to put the file in the message.

10. Add a subject to the message.

Be sure to add a sequence number, such as (1/3), if you split the file into several segments.

T I P

11. Click **Send** to post the message.

12. Repeat steps 4 through 11 to post all segments of the file.

NETSCAPE

Based on Netscape Navigator 3.0.

N O T E

TO DOWNLOAD A FILE FROM THE WEB

1. Go to the appropriate Web site.

2. Click the link to the desired file to open a common Save As dialog box.

Netscape tries to use its helper applications to display any file that you select. If it doesn't know what helper application to use, it displays the dialog box shown below:

Unknown File Type	☒

You have started to download a file of type application/x-navi-animation
Click "More Info" to learn how to extend Navigator's capabilities.

| More Info | Pick App... | Save File... | Cancel |

Click **Save File** to open the Save As dialog box.

T I P   If Netscape doesn't recognize the file type at all, it will try to display the file as a text file instead of downloading it. This is probably not what you want. See the procedure called "To define a file type" for directions on getting Netscape to recognize the file type.

3. Choose a directory for the file and click **OK**.

    A progress dialog box keeps you informed while the file downloads.

4. Sign off, if desired. You don't need to be online for the remaining steps.

5. Decode the file, if necessary.

6. Unzip the file, if necessary.

7. If any executable files were added to your system, scan them for viruses.

To DOWNLOAD A FILE FROM FTP

Convert the FTP address into a URL by inserting ftp:// in front of it, as in ftp://ftp.microsoft.com. Then follow the procedure for downloading from a Web site.

To DEFINE A FILE TYPE

1. Choose **Options|General Preferences** to open the dialog box below:

![Preferences dialog box showing the Helpers tab with file type, Action, and Extensions columns. Below are fields for File / MIME Type: x-conference, Subtype: x-cooltalk, File Extensions: ICE, and Action radio buttons including Launch the Application with path d:\netscape\CoolTalk\COOLTALK.EXE]

2. Click the **Helpers** tab to open the Helpers page.
3. Type the file's extension in the **File Extensions** box, replacing whatever is already there.
4. For **Action,** select either **Save to Disk** or **Unknown: Ask User.**

T I P

If you choose **Save to Disk**, Netscape will automatically save files of this type to your hard disk. If you choose **Unknown: Ask User**, Netscape will always ask you what you want to do with a file of this type.

5. Click **Create New Type** to open the dialog box shown below:

Configure New Mime Type	☒

| Mime Type: | application |
| Mime SubType: | octet-stream |

| OK | Cancel |

6. Unless you know the Mime type and subtype for the file, use **application/octet-stream** (the default type) as shown in the above example.

7. Click **OK** to close the dialog box and create the new type. You'll see the type appear in the list box.

8. Click **OK** to close the Preferences dialog box.

EUDORA LIGHT

TO ATTACH A FILE TO EMAIL

1. Click the **New Message** icon to open a blank letter.

2. Fill out the address and subject and write a note to accompany the file.

3. Choose **Message|Attach File**.

   Eudora Light opens a browse dialog box where you can locate and select the file to be attached.

4. Select the file and click **OK**.

   Eudora Light attaches the file to the letter.

5. Click **Send** to send the file.

N O T E

You have to be online to send the file.

To DOWNLOAD A FILE FROM EMAIL

Attached files are downloaded automatically as soon as you retrieve letters in Eudora Light.

THE MICROSOFT NETWORK

To DOWNLOAD A FILE FROM A NEWSGROUP

1. From MSN Central, choose Edit|GoTo|Other Location and enter "newsgroups" to get to the Newsgroups window.
2. Locate the newsgroup that you want to download from.

You can go directly to the desired newsgroup from MSN Central by entering news:newsgroup in the Go To Service dialog. For example, to go to comp.dos, you would enter news:comp.dos.

T I P

3. Open the message that you want to download from.

   The message should include the uuencoded data, as shown below:

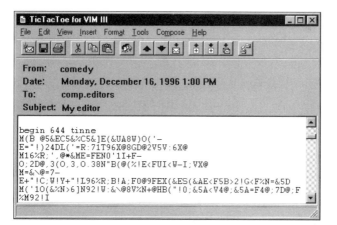

4. Choose FilelSave As to save the message as a file on your hard drive.

5. You might want to sign out before completing the rest of these steps.

6. uudecode the file.

7. Unzip the file, if necessary.

8. Virus scan any executable files that you added to your system in this procedure.

UPLOADING A FILE TO A NEWSGROUP

1. If the file is binary, uuencode it, splitting it into several small files if necessary.

2. Sign on to MSN.

3. From MSN Central, choose EditlGoTolOther Location and enter "newsgroups" to get to the Newsgroups window.

4. Locate the newsgroup that you want to upload to.

You can go directly to the desired newsgroup from MSN Central by entering news:newsgroup in the Go To Service dialog. For example, to go to comp.dos, you would enter news:comp.dos.

T I P

5. Choose ComposelNew Message (Ctrl+N) or click the New Message icon (if the toolbar is showing) to open a New Message dialog, shown below:

```
┌─────────────────────────────────────────────────────┐
│ ▣ New Message                               _ □ ✕    │
│ File  Edit  View  Insert  Format  Tools  Compose  Help│
│ ┌──┬──┬──┐ ┌──┬──┬──┐ ┌──┐                           │
│ │▣ │▦ │▤ │ │✂ │▦ │▩ │ │▨ │                           │
│ └──┴──┴──┘ └──┴──┴──┘ └──┘                           │
│ To:       comp.fonts                                 │
│ Subject: ┌──────────────────────────────────────────┐│
│          └──────────────────────────────────────────┘│
│ │                                                     │
│ │                                                     │
│ │                                                     │
│ │                                                     │
│ │                                                     │
│ │                                                     │
│ │                                                     │
│ │                                                     │
│ │                                                    ╱│
└─────────────────────────────────────────────────────┘
```

6. Open the uuencoded file in Notepad (or any text editor).

7. Copy the text of the uuencoded file into the new message.

8. Give the new message a subject.

Don't forget to add a sequence number, such as (1/3), if this is a multipart file.

T I P

9. Click the Post tool to post the message.

To download a file from the Web

You must have set up your copy of MSN to use Internet Explorer. Choose Tools|Connection Settings, click the Access Numbers button, and choose Internet and the Microsoft Network.

T I P

1. Sign on to MSN and start Internet Explorer.

2. Click the Open icon to open the Open Internet Address dialog.

3. Type the URL and press Enter to display the site.

4. Click the file that you want to download.

5. A dialog asks what you want to do with the file, as shown below:

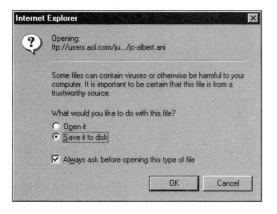

T I P

If Internet Explorer knows how to display the file, it will do so. In that case, you need to choose File|Save As to download the file.

6. Select Save to Disk and click OK.

A common Windows Save As dialog appears so that you can designate where you want to save the file.

7. Select the desired directory and click Save.

A progress dialog keeps you informed while the file downloads.

8. Sign off, if desired. You don't need to be online for the remaining steps.

9. Decode the file, if necessary.

10.   Unzip the file, if necessary.

11. If any executable files were added to your system, scan them for viruses.

To download a file from the Web

The process is the same as downloading from the Web except you use an ftp address as your URL, as in ftp://ftp.microsoft.com.

INDEX